Warrior • 41

Knight Hospitaller (2)

1306–1565

David Nicolle • Illustrated by Christa Hook

271.791
Nic

First published in Great Britain in 2001 by Osprey Publishing,
Midland House, West Way, Botley, Oxford OX2 0PH, UK
443 Park Avenue South, New York, NY 10016, USA
Email: info@ospreypublishing.com

CIP Data for this publication is available from the British Library

ISBN-10: 1-84176-215-6
ISBN-13: 978-1-84176-215-9

Editor: Nikolai Bogdanovic
Design: Ken Vail Graphic Design, Cambridge, UK
Index by Alison Worthington
Typeset in Helvetica Neue and ITC New Baskerville
Originated by Magnet Herlequin, Uxbridge, UK
Printed in China through World Print Ltd.

06 07 08 09 10 12 11 10 9 8 7 6 5 4 3

FOR A CATALOGUE OF ALL BOOKS PUBLISHED BY OSPREY MILITARY AND
AVIATION PLEASE CONTACT:

NORTH AMERICA
Osprey Direct, C/o Random House Distribution Center,
400 Hahn Road, Westminster, MD 21157, USA
E-mail: info@ospreydirect.com

ALL OTHER REGIONS
Osprey Direct UK, P.O. Box 140, Wellingborough,
Northants, NN8 2FA, UK
E-mail: info@ospreydirect.co.uk

www.ospreypublishing.com

Artist's note

Readers may care to note that the original paintings from
which the colour plates in this book were prepared are
available for private sale. All reproduction copyright
whatsoever is retained by the Publishers. All enquiries
should be addressed to:

Scorpio Gallery, PO Box 475, Hailsham, East Sussex,
BN27 2SL, UK.

The Publishers regret that they can enter into no
correspondence upon this matter.

Dedication

In Memory of Squadron Leader Mohammed Abd al-Hamid
Abu Zeid, one of Egypt's forgotten heroes.

CONTENTS

KNIGHT HOSPITALLER (2) 1306–1565

THE KNIGHTS GET A NEW HOME

When Foulques de Villaret was elected master of the Hospitallers in 1305 the Order entered a more active phase. Both Foulques and the master of the Templars favoured an attack on Egypt using Cyprus, the Hospitallers' new headquarters, as a base. Pope Clement V had a high opinion of both masters' crusading expertise but their opinions differed. Both wrote reports outlining what they regarded as the best way of regaining the Holy Land.

Whereas the Templar memorandum was brief and confident, that by Foulques de Villaret was longer, more carefully argued and subtle. It emphasised prudence and careful preparation, suggesting that a series of small-scale operations over a prolonged period would be more effective in wearing down Mamluk power than the sort of all-out crusading invasion that had so often come to grief. The widest possible support should be sought, including alliances with the Armenian kingdom of Cilicia and the Mongols, though this vision was out of date since the Mongols were in the process of converting to Islam. Above all Foulques emphasised the need for adequate finances, which is ironic since the rival Templars got the historical reputation of being the 'bankers' among the military orders.

Realism probably prompted the Hospitallers to conquer the Byzantine island of Rhodes, the secure and independent base – something that the Teutonic Knights were already doing in the Baltic and which the doomed Templars never achieved. While the Templars faced increasing hostility from the King of France, there was tension between the Hospitallers and the King of Cyprus, so it is not surprising that the Order looked for an alternative home. Armenian Cilicia had few harbours, an unhealthy coast, was vulnerable to Turkish raids and was uncomfortably close to the

Renart the Fox during a dispute between a Hospitaller (left) and a Templar (right). This early 14th-century illustration is from a copy of a satirical tale that criticises both Orders. (*Renart de Nouvel*, Bibliothèque Nationale, Ms. Fr. 372, f. 59, Paris, France)

The walls of Silifke castle on the southern coast of Turkey. This great fortress was built by the Hospitallers. (Turkish Tourist Information Department)

regional superpowers of Mamluk Syria–Egypt and Mongol Iraq–Iran. Rhodes, however, was an island and the seas were still controlled by Christians. It also overlooked the trade route from the Black Sea, which not only supplied Egypt with wood and iron but also with those Turkish slaves who formed the backbone of the Mamluk army and state.

The Hospitaller leaders had argued for a trade blockade of Egypt. Now their possession of Rhodes might enable them and their crusading allies to impose it. Piracy was endemic throughout the Aegean. Meanwhile Western merchants and pirates were already active around Rhodes, which Venice also coveted. More recently Turkish forces had seized part of the island. So the Hospitallers were entering a chaotic region and found themselves facing two main enemies: Muslim Turks and Orthodox Christian Greeks, whom the Hospitallers, as Latin or Catholic Christians, regarded as schismatics.

Once established, however, the Hospitallers not only acquired a new convent or headquarters but also a new role. As a slightly later account of the conquest of Rhodes states:

The Grand Master Foulques de Villaret and the valiant Brothers of the Hospital gave thanks to God and to the Virgin Mary for the wealth and abundance which had come to them. They built a great castle and conquered all around, collecting many fine men who wished to come to Rhodes to reconnoitre and to colonize the island. Then they had many places in Anatolia submit to their authority which gave them tribute.

Unfortunately de Villaret behaved like a despotic sovereign rather than an elected leader, provoking a rebellion in 1317, and the crisis was only resolved after the Pope intervened. De Villaret resigned, a new master, Helion de Villeneuve, took over and the Order was able to focus on its new role. The Order offered land to would-be colonisers in return for military service, and although efforts to carve out a presence on the Anatolian mainland failed, other islands were seized from Lerro (now called Léros) in the north to Castelrosso (now called Kastellórizon) in the south, while Scarpanto (now called Kárpathos) in the west was handed over to Venice. Meanwhile the Hospitallers' great rivals, the Templars, had been disbanded and most of their assets transferred to the Hospitallers.

The conquest of Rhodes had been an impressive combined sea–land operation, but it took the Order a long time to become truly 'naval minded' and in fact their activity was limited for many decades. Nevertheless, Rhodes now dominated several hundred kilometres of the Turkish coast. The nearby Turkish *beylik* (small, independent Islamic state) of Mentese was virtually denied access to the sea and so the main centre of Turkish naval operations shifted northwards to the beylik of Aydin. In 1344 the Hospitallers joined other crusaders in seizing Aydin's main port of Smyrna (now Izmir), so the focus of Turkish naval operations again shifted northwards to the rapidly expanding Ottoman emirate, or sultanate as it became, which crossed the Dardanelles and started expanding into Europe.

Meanwhile the Hospitallers still focused on the powerful Mamluk sultanate and in 1365 took part in a devastating but largely pointless attack on the great Egyptian port of Alexandria. As crusader territory shrank elsewhere in Greece and the Aegean, so the importance of Rhodes rose. Hospitaller relations with the Mamluks also improved and developed into something approaching an alliance during the 15th century.

Relations between the Hospitallers and the people of Rhodes were dominated by two factors: the religious gulf separating the dominant Catholic Hospitallers and the subordinate Orthodox Greeks, and their mutual concern for defence. In the city of Rhodes, for example, the local population was expelled to a neighbouring suburb which was, however, given a strong defensive wall. The Hospitallers also insisted that the local Orthodox Church recognise the supremacy of the Pope. Eventually the urban Greeks did so, though the rural Greek villagers apparently did not. All were integrated into a feudal and defence structure that the Hospitallers imposed upon their islands, yet the different status of Greeks and Latins was clearly shown in the size of the estates they were granted.

Many Greek families were bound by a hereditary *servitudo marina* that obliged them to man the Order's galleys, and this was only abolished in 1462 when so many men fled the island that women could not find husbands to marry. In fact Greek hostility to Latins, including the Hospitallers, ran very deep throughout the Aegean region. Nevertheless Rhodes prospered under Hospitaller rule and became a major transit point in the slave trade from the Black Sea. Many European families settled on Rhodes and the other Hospitaller-held islands, including mercenary soldiers, privateers with their ships and crews, lawyers, bankers, gunners, swordsmiths, armourers, all sorts of other craftsmen and medical staff for the famous infirmary. Jews were listed among the physicians, surgeons, apothecaries and craftsmen while there were also Armenians, Cypriots and Maronite Christian Syrians.

One of the most unusual effigies in England portrays an unknown knight in a monk's habit worn over mail armour. Was he a member of one of the military orders or did his take monastic vows towards the end of his life? (*In situ*, church, Conington, England; author's photograph)

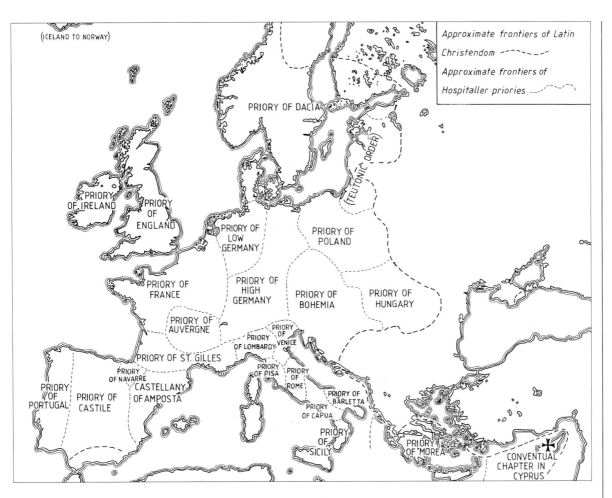

(ICELAND TO NORWAY)

Approximate frontiers of Latin
Christendom ------
Approximate frontiers of
Hospitaller priories -----

PRIORY OF DACIA

PRIORY
OF IRELAND

PRIORY
OF
ENGLAND

(TEUTONIC ORDER)

PRIORY OF
LOW
GERMANY

PRIORY OF
POLAND

PRIORY OF
FRANCE

PRIORY OF
HIGH
GERMANY

PRIORY OF
BOHEMIA

PRIORY OF
HUNGARY

PRIORY OF
AUVERGNE

PRIORY
OF
VENICE

PRIORY
OF LOMBARDY

PRIORY OF ST. GILLES

PRIORY
OF NAVARRE

PRIORY
OF PISA

PRIORY
OF
ROME

CASTELLANY
OF AMPOSTA

PRIORY
OF
PORTUGAL

PRIORY OF
CASTILE

PRIORY OF
BARLETTA

PRIORY
OF CAPUA

PRIORY
OF
SICILY

PRIORY
OF MOREA

CONVENTUAL
CHAPTER IN
CYPRUS

**Hospitaller priories c.1300. The
territory of the Teutonic Order in
the Baltic was not included
within a Hospitaller priory.**

CHRONOLOGY

1306	Hospitallers begin invasion of Byzantine island of Rhodes.
1309	Hospitaller headquarters moved to Rhodes.
1312	Suppression of the Templars; most of their estates transferred to the Hospitallers; Hospitaller naval victory over the Turks.
1317	Foulques de Villaret deposed 1317 as master (formally abdicated 1319); Order under a temporary lieutenant, Gerard de Pins.
1319	Hospitaller and Genoese fleet destroys Turkish flotilla off Ephesus; island of Lango lost to the Turks, but Lerro gained from Byzantines; Hélion de Villeneuve becomes master.
c.1337	Hospitallers regain Lango.
1344	Hospitallers join Papal League in the capture of Izmir.
1346	Dieudonné de Gozon becomes master.
1348	Plague hits Rhodes.
1353	Pierre de Corneillan becomes master.
1355	Roger de Pins becomes master.
1359	Hospitaller ships join others in defeating Turkish flotilla off the Dardanelles.
1361	Hospitallers join Cypriots attacking Antalya.
1365	Hospitallers join crusade in devastating Alexandria.
1365	Raimond Bèrenger becomes master.
1374	Hospitallers accept responsibility for defence of crusader-held Izmir.
1374	Robert de Juilly becomes master.
1376–81	Disastrous Hospitaller invasion of Despotate of Epiros.
1377	Juan Fernandez de Heredia becomes master.

1383	'Anti-Master' Riccardo Caracciolo appointed by Pope Urban VI but not acknowledged in Rhodes (resigns in 1395).
1396	Hospitallers take part in crusade, which is defeated by Ottomans at Nicopolis; Philibert de Naillac becomes master.
1397	Hospitallers occupy Corinth.
1401	Crusader Prince of Achaea attacks Hospitaller possessions on Greek mainland.
1402	Timur-i Lenk captures Izmir.
1403	Hospitaller treaty with the Mamluk sultanate of Egypt; crusader Duke of Athens attacks Hospitaller possessions on Greek mainland.
1404	Hospitallers abandon Corinth.
c.1407	Hospitallers take and fortify Bodrum.
1421	Antonio de Fluvía becomes master.
1426	Mamluks impose suzerainty on Cyprus.
1437	Jean de Lastic becomes master.
1443	Mamluks briefly capture Castellorizo.
1444	Unsuccessful Mamluk invasion of Rhodes; Hospitaller peace treaty with Mamluks renewed.

ABOVE **Mertola castle in southern Portugal was held by the Hospitallers for many years following the conquest of this region from the Moors. (author's photograph)**

BELOW **Effigy of Ugo de Cervellon, who died in 1334. He wears an old-fashioned form of armour apparently consisting entirely of mail. It would also have been used by many Hospitaller brethren-in-arms in this part of Europe. (*In situ*, Hospitaller Church, Villafranca del Panadés, Spain)**

1451	Hospitallers attack Karaman in alliance with Mamluks.
1454	Jacques de Milly becomes master.
1455	Ottomans raid Rhodes.
1461	Raimundo Zacosta becomes master.
1467	Giovan Battista Orsini becomes master.
1476	Pierre d'Aubusson becomes master.
1480	Unsuccessful Ottoman invasion of Rhodes.
1503	Emery d'Amboise becomes master.
1512	Guy de Blanchefort becomes master.
1513	Fabrizio del Carretto becomes master.
1521	Philippe Villiers de l'Isle Adam becomes master.
1522	Ottomans conquer Rhodes; Hospitaller headquarters moved to Italy.
1528	Hospitallers help defend Spanish-held Tripoli.
1530	Hospitaller headquarters moved to Malta.
1531	Hospitaller expedition briefly captures Modon in Greece.
1534	Pietrino del Ponte becomes master.
1535	Didier de Tholon Sainte-Jalle becomes master.
1536	Juan de Homedes y Coscon becomes master.
1541	Hospitallers take part in unsuccessful Spanish attack on Algiers.
1551	Hospitallers lose Tripoli.
1553	Claude de la Sengle becomes master.
1557	Jean Parisot de la Valette becomes master.
1565	Unsuccessful Ottoman invasion of Malta.

Christian warrior saints were a popular subject in medieval European art, and this Italian *acquamanile* or drinks pourer in the form of St George gives an excellent impression of what a Hospitaller brother knight would have looked like around 1340. (Bargello Museum, inv. R.372, Florence, Italy)

RECRUITMENT

Recruitment to the Order of Hospitallers during the 14th to mid-16th centuries was based on the systems that had been used in the 12th and 13th centuries. However, the world from which these men were drawn was changing and this was reflected in Hospitaller recruitment. Throughout most of western Europe the military aristocracy retained its role in military leadership. Yet the prestige of this aristocracy was under threat from a rising middle class, and this led to a defensive resurgence of the old chivalric ethos. Meanwhile the 14th and 15th centuries also saw widespread criticism of a supposed decline in knighthood and chivalry. Given this crisis of identity within the knightly elite, and what seems to have been a greater number of men than women in some parts of Europe, the motivation of Hospitaller recruits is liable to have been mixed.

Though the dissolution of the Templars provided the Hospitallers with increased wealth, ex-Templars were forbidden from joining the Hospitallers. Declining enthusiasm for the crusade not only reduced the flow of recruits but also reduced the donations of land and other assets. Indeed many of the dwindling number of patrons only gave to the Order in return for expensive chantry priests who would pray for the souls of the donor for ever. Furthermore Hungarian success in containing Ottoman expansion on land meant that new crusades were often seen as unnecessary, while in the Mediterranean Venice was more interested in maintaining peace with the Ottoman sultanate than in seeking confrontation. Even the hysterical calls for a crusade by those who spread stories of 'the terrible Turk' may have backfired by creating fear of the 'invincible' Ottomans, and it was not until the Hospitallers of Rhodes defeated a major Ottoman attack in 1480 that the Order saw a serious increase in recruitment.

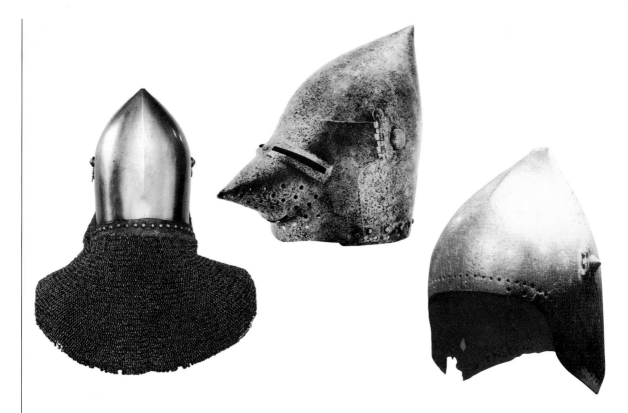

Many who joined the Hospitallers probably did so to find a career rather than for reasons of crusading enthusiasm. There was little scope for religious contemplation within the Order and, apart from the small number of men who were sent on rotation to Rhodes, little scope for military action. Even there life offered less adventure than, for example, in the warlike Baltic outposts of the rival Order of Teutonic Knights. For most Hospitaller brethren life was one of administrative duty, but it was secure and offered reasonable status. Only a tiny clique of senior men, often drawn from noble families, jockeyed for position, financial rewards and prestige at the top of the Order.

During the 12th and 13th centuries the Order of the Hospitallers had been dominated by men from southern France, and Frenchmen continued to dominate the Order throughout most of the 14th century. Information on the numbers of brethren in the central convent in Cyprus and Rhodes from 1302 to 1522 shows an increasing number from Spain and Italy, but only small numbers from England and Germany, plus a few from Portugal, Scotland, Denmark and Hungary. Rivalry between the *langues* or 'tongues' within the Order was intense, and the way that Master Roger de Pins used his position to advance his own nation caused a reaction in 1374 with the election of the first non-Provençal master in 78 years. This was followed by a comparable period during which men of Spanish origin almost took over the Order.

The Hospitallers faced different problems of recruitment in different countries. In England, for example, there was widespread anti-papal feeling because the popes were seen as pro-French during the Hundred Years War, and to some extent this resentment rubbed off on the Hospitallers. English interest in the Order increased following a visit

LEFT **Rear view of a late 14th-century Italian bascinet with its aventail. (Royal Armouries, Leeds, England)**
CENTRE **Bascinet from the Château d'Avusy near Geneva, c.1400, probably Italian. (Musée d'Art et d'Histoire, inv. 65d; SWI 622, Geneva, Switzerland)**
RIGHT **Northern Italian bascinet without its visor, c.1390. (Pinacoteca Comunale, San Gimignano, Italy)**

OPPOSITE (FROM TOP TO BOTTOM)
A **Seal of the grand commander of the hospital**
B **Seal of the grand priory of England**
C **Seal of the Hospitaller priory of France**
D **Seal of the Hospitaller priory of Provence**
E **Seal of the Hospitaller grand commander of Spain.**

to Rhodes by the Earl of Derby, subsequently King Henry IV, but in 1445 a meeting of the English langue in Rhodes was still attended by only 11 brothers.

The Hospitallers' situation was different in Slav lands and Hungary where western European feudal structures were a relatively new introduction. There was also resentment among indigenous aristocracies against the influence wielded by foreign Hospitaller elites. Both factors inhibited local recruitment. In Italy relations between Venice and the Hospitallers, who had fundamentally different attitudes towards the Islamic world, meant that very few Venetians joined the Order. In the Iberian peninsula the Hospitallers faced competition from local Spanish military orders for recruits, donations and royal patronage. A shocking degree of nepotism also developed among senior Hospitallers drawn from the Iberian aristocracies, particularly in Portugal.

Novitiates and those *donats* who were awaiting admission as novitiates still lived in Hospitaller houses, although, as the size of the Order's communities in Europe declined, a larger proportion did their novitiate in Rhodes. Here the Order faced other manpower problems. During the mid-14th century there were so few men of recognised European origin that the Chapter ruled that those with Latin fathers but Greek mothers should be considered legally Latin. In 1424 Latin residents of Rhodes were allowed to enter the Order if they got letters of naturalisation from their father's home state back in Europe, which would seem to exclude second-generation settlers. In 1478 some local Rhodian Greeks requested permission to join but this was denied.

The process of initiation into the Order also changed little, as is shown in a description of the admission of the King of Aragon's eldest son, Jaime, in 1319. During this church service Father Arnau de Soler, the Preceptor of Barcelona, sat before the altar holding the Gospels and a cross. Jaime, dressed as a Hospitaller but without the characteristic mantle, knelt before him placing his hands on the book and cross. Father Arnau explained a brother's obligations and said that the new entrant would have a probationary year. After making his vows of obedience Jaime rose, and placed the book and cross on Arnau's knees. The preceptor then received him as a brother, placing the black mantle with its white cross on his shoulders. New members were normally assigned to a house under the preceptor's obedience and were often allotted a squire, two servants, a horse and a pack animal.

Brother knights had always been more influential than brother sergeants, and this became even more obvious during the 14th and 15th centuries. The aristocratisation of the Order was also reflected in a statute or law that defined the number of noble quarterings that an aspiring brother knight needed in his coat-of-arms. In Italy it was only four because many decades of intermarriage between noble and wealthy bourgeois families made it unwise to look too deeply into a young aristocrat's origins. In France and Spain eight noble quarterings would be required, whereas in Germany it was no fewer than 16. Recruitment to the Order became even more selective after 1565, with a concern that recruits not only have several generations of the purest noble blood but also no taint of Protestant heresy.

Little is known about the careers of Hospitaller brother sergeants. Most still seem to have been recruited from peasants or urban

ABOVE **The effigy of an unknown Aragonese knight from the second half of the 14th century, a period when Spanish influence was growing within the Hospitaller Order. (*In situ*, Hospitaller Church, Villafranca del Panadés, Spain)**

LEFT **Relief carving of a warrior saint, probably St George, above the carved coats-of-arms of Hospitaller brethren and perhaps *donats*. (*In situ*, Bodrum Castle, Turkey; photograph Mary Orr)**

craftsmen, though some may have come from knightly families who were too poor to join as brother knights. Such men took their orders from the knights and many of these knights would, at various times in their careers, have found themselves in command of Hospitaller troops who were not brethren of the Order. These included *turcopoles* recruited from local Greeks and other non-Latins. In fact the more recently arrived Syrian Christians and Armenians seem to have been regarded as more reliable soldiers than the Rhodian Greeks. Hospitaller brother knights would have similarly served alongside, and often commanded, the large numbers of European mercenaries who came to Rhodes. Other non-brethren included specialists, among them the Englishman Stephen Ward, who became master of the Rhodian arsenal in the mid-15th century.

ORGANISATION, STRUCTURE AND FINANCE

The main purpose of the organisational structure of the Hospitaller Order was to maintain the garrisons on Rhodes and the other islands. It was reformed on several occasions, but the biggest change was probably the acquisition of ex-Templar properties following the fall of the Templars in the early 14th century. On the other hand it sometimes cost the Hospitallers a great deal of money to actually get these estates handed over. The Order was now a highly bureaucratic organisation with every priory keeping detailed records of rents, incomes and properties, the entire system being directed by the master and his household in Rhodes. He himself acted with the agreement of the chapter general, or headquarters' council, which was theoretically his superior. In reality many 14th-century masters were elderly and well meaning but somewhat ineffective.

The Order's possessions in Europe were grouped into regions called priories in the 12th century, but now a system of langues or broadly linguistic 'tongues' appeared in the east. Initially there were five langues, later increased to seven, each of which was of equal status and was represented in the chapter general. A langue was headed by a *pilier* or 'pillar' who, from 1320 onwards, also held one of the great offices of the Order. Thus the grand commander came from Provence, the marshal from Auvergne, the hospitaller from France, the drapier from Spain, the admiral from Italy and the turcopolier from England. Nothing was specifically set aside for the German langue, nor was the role of treasurer attached to a specific langue. From the start of the 15th century the office of drapier's lieutenant was traditionally given to a Spaniard and from then on each pilier could also claim a priory and its revenues when one fell vacant.

The primary task of brethren in the east was of course military and each langue was given a section of the fortifications of the city of Rhodes to defend. Meanwhile the number of brethren in Rhodes increased as the Order's finances stabilised. By 1480 the garrison of Rhodes consisted of around 450 brother knights, 150 brother sergeants, and 1,500 to 2,000 other soldiers excluding local militias. Nevertheless, some of the brethren were too old to fight, while others were in different castles or

ABOVE LEFT **The Master of the Order, Pierre d'Aubusson, exhorting his troops during the Ottoman Turkish siege of the city of Rhodes in 1480, as illustrated in Guillaume Caoursin's late 15th-century account of the siege. Note the Hospitallers' defensive artillery arranged in batteries of four or more guns. (***Obsidionis Rhodie Urbis Descriptio***, Bibliotheque Nationale, Ms. Lat. 6067, f.37v, Paris, France)**

ABOVE RIGHT **The warrior saint in this mid-14th-century northern Italian wall painting wears much the same surcoat as that of a brother knight of the Hospitallers. His arm and leg armour is of hardened leather. (***In situ***, Avio Castle, Italy; author's photograph)**

aboard ship. A partial roll-call of brother knights and sergeants at the start of the final 1522 siege lists 290 brother knights, 15 donats, about 300 brother sergeants-at-arms, plus around 950 European sailors or soldiers and several thousand Rhodian militia. The garrisons of other Hospitaller outposts in the Aegean were naturally much smaller but every brother knight in Rhodes had to spend at least one year in the Lango garrison.

The Hospitallers' extensive possessions in western Europe provided their main financial strength. Here the chief problems were distance and the slowness of medieval communications, so the Order attempted to delegate authority. Unfortunately the system of visitation by representatives from the central convent was clearly inadequate and many priors failed to visit the convent as often as they should have. The result was widespread inefficiency and corruption.

Since the primary purpose of European estates was to support the fighting men in Rhodes, they tried to make the best use of land and other assets. Sometimes this involved 'development' in a modern sense, as well as the colonisation of both Slav, Hungarian and Celtic frontier regions. In the Iberian peninsula the Hospitallers had often been given lands and castles in return for their participation in warfare against the neighbouring Muslims of al-Andalus, but elsewhere in Spain Hospitaller property was associated with the Pilgrim Road to Santiago, providing hospices rather than military protection. In 1247 King Bela IV of Hungary granted the Hospitallers the Severin area in what is now south-western Romania, yet there is no evidence that they helped defend

Severin or Hungary against the Mongol invasion a few years later. Instead the Aegean remained the Order's priority until the fall of Rhodes in 1522.

The 25 priories and grand commanderies now formed the middle level of Hospitaller administration, with the langues above and the commanderies or preceptories below. A preceptor or commander headed a convent, though those in charge of houses of brother clerics or priests rather than knights or sergeants were normally, and confusingly called priors. Preceptors or commanders could be brother knights, brother sergeants or brother priests. Some were appointed for life, though most only served a short term before being moved on to another convent. As a result some became highly experienced and valued administrators. It must also be borne in mind that many if not most of these same men had either served as active soldiers in Rhodes or could find themselves summoned east to join the garrison. Though they were rarely soft-living bureaucrats, sexual immorality seems to have been common, though violent disorder was rare.

The other brethren in the *domus* or 'house' administered the surrounding properties through chapters or meetings usually held once a week. Such 14th-century Hospitaller houses varied considerably in size, and a detailed survey, ordered by the Pope in 1338 as part of widespread reforms, shows that the biggest in England had ten brethren while most had only two or three. Some houses in mainland Europe were considerable larger. The number of local people dependent on a Hospitaller preceptory as their feudal lord varied but could be up to 5,000. There were also regional variations in the proportion of brother knights to other brethren.

Few brethren played a military role outside the Aegean and to some extent Iberia. Scottish and Welsh rulers were patrons of the Order, as were English kings, and there is no evidence that the Hospitallers had any military role against highland Welsh or highland Scots. On the rare occasions that the Hospitaller prior in Ireland was involved in military action, he did so in defence of the king's realm, like any other loyal 'liege man'. Hospitallers in the Iberian peninsula did play some military role but this was not always against the Muslim Andalusians to the south. Those in Aragon quite often found themselves caught up in wars against the fellow Christian kingdom of Castile or were involved in Aragon's empire-building elsewhere in the Mediterranean.

The effigy of Juan Fernandez de Heredia, master of the Hospitallers, showing his family coat-of-arms quartered with those of the Order. (Caspe, destroyed during the Spanish Civil War)

The bridge at Puenta de la Reinha where the pilgrim roads through Navarre and Aragon joined. The Hospitallers' possessions in this town were among their most important in the Iberian peninsula. (Author's photograph)

Normally a grand preceptor was in charge of Hospitaller priories in Germany and the rest of central Europe, sometimes including Scandinavia, but the area of his responsibility varied. The lack of centralised monarchies in Germany and Bohemia also helped the Hospitallers to acquire estates and castles, but this tended to draw them into local political rivalries. Meanwhile the ordinary brethren of the Order in eastern Germany and neighbouring Slav kingdoms were involved in economic development and colonisation. Once again Hospitaller numbers were small and included both German and Slav brethren, there being around 30 brethren in Pomerania during the first half of the 14th century.

Circumstances in the vast kingdom of Hungary were again different. Despite its distinctive character, the priory of Hungary did not form a separate langue and was instead sometimes part of the German langue and sometimes part of the Italian. A large part of the Hungarian kingdom also fell within the priory of Bohemia. The first Hospitaller properties in Hungary were concentrated in the north-west of the country, but with the acquisition of ex-Templar estates the Order's centre of gravity shifted southwards, towards the Adriatic coast of what is now Croatia. The most isolated of all Hospitaller priories was that of Dacia or Scandinavia, which was so far from both Rome and Rhodes that its limited revenues rarely reached the central convent.

The Order of the Hospitallers had an effective system of internal consultation, decision making and justice, though it would be wrong to describe it as democratic. It was instead a kind of oligarchy dominated by the most experienced men from each langue. As a result legislation within the Order, known as *stabilimenta*, was discussed by the conventual chapter, which also acted like a supreme court. Following a statute drawn up under the mastership of de Naillac, and perhaps reflecting the spread of consultative if not democratic feelings in later medieval Europe, there were more meetings of this conventual chapter during the 15th century than ever before.

On a more day-to-day basis the Order was preoccupied with its finances. Though hugely wealthy it incurred huge expenses, and the cost of transporting food, raw materials, armaments and horses from western Europe to Rhodes was immense, as was the cost of maintaining the island's fortifications. On the other hand Hospitaller brethren also dealt with minor sums. In 1409 a severe financial crisis in Rhodes was at least alleviated by the arrival of some Venetian galleys bringing no less than 5,000 ducats from England. Of this 1,900 was spent on Bodrum castle, 1,000 on mercenary troops, 300 on stipends for the brethren and 600 for their food. At the other end of the financial scale an Englishmen from York, John Pigot Esquire, gave £2 in his will for Bodrum castle's fabric and defences in 1429. The hugely valuable gifts that the Prior of Provence sent to Rhodes at the start of the 16th century included the famous *Rhodes Missal*, but he also sent more immediately practical objects, ranging from four bronze cannon and their carriages to 500 shares in the Genoese Bank of St George.

BELOW LEFT **Pierre de Bosredon as he appeared in his own late 15th-century *Book of the Hours*. By this time the presbyters of Hospitaller houses in western Europe lived much as did other members of the local aristocracy. (*Hours of the Virgin Mary of Father Pierre de Bosredon*, Pierpont Morgan Library, Ms. Glazier 55, f.125, New York, USA)**

BELOW RIGHT **The Street of the Knights in the inner quarter of the city of Rhodes, which was reserved for the Hospitaller Order itself, showing the Auberge de France with its turrets and carved doorway. (Photograph Greek Tourist Department)**

When King Edward III of England defaulted on his debts he caused the collapse of the Hospitallers' Italian bank, wiping out their financial reserve of 360,000 florins. Under these circumstances it is hardly surprising that the Order undertook major financial reforms. In 1358 the collection of all dues was taken away from priors and placed in the hands of a receiver allocated to each priory. In 1373 a detailed survey of all Hospitaller properties also looked at the numbers, values and residents of all priories. The result made dismal reading, with diminished incomes, abandoned churches, falling numbers of brethren, too many priests, elderly brothers and absentee preceptors. The purge that followed removed many of the easygoing commandery households, replacing them with a more efficient structure in which the commander was often the only 'professed brother' in each domus or house. As a result revenues almost doubled.

In 1410 a chapter general held at Aix in southern France rather than Rhodes resulted in further reforms, mostly to remove fraud, restore the authority of the master and attempt to ensure that brethren obeyed the statutes of the Order. Another perhaps much needed reform concerned the statutes themselves. These had accumulated over the centuries, resulting in confusion, disagreement and contradiction, so the revised statutes were arranged systematically. Then there was the question of language. The Hospitallers' original 12th-century statutes were written in Provençal. In 1357 these had been translated into Latin, which was understood throughout Europe. The revised statutes were also drawn up in Latin, and in 1567 Italian finally became the official language of the Order.

Two men wearing Hospitaller robes in symbolic portrayal of the hierarchy of power, painted by Andrea da Firenze in 1355. The white-bearded Hospitaller is believed to be the master, Juan Fernandez de Heredia. (*In situ*, Spanish Chapel, Santa Maria Novella, Florence, Italy)

MOTIVATION AND MORALE

In Rhodes the fighting arm of the Order created a remarkable and rather romantic haven of chivalry at a time when the ideals of chivalry were under threat elsewhere in Europe. Here the Hospitallers continued to see themselves as *propugnacula fidee* or 'bulwarks of the faith' in the east. Rhodes itself became a sort of idealised Arthurian *Isle de Gramarye*, a citadel where true knights could follow the code of true chivalry. This resulted in legends emerging around some Hospitaller masters such as Dieudonné de Gozon. He came to Rhodes as a young man and was said to have slain a 'wicked worm' or dragon that had been eating young maidens and had already killed several knights. The probable reality behind this legend was the young de Gozon's training of hunting dogs to find and kill a troublesome snake. Meanwhile Hospitaller masters tried to fill their court with the noblest blood in Christendom while also spreading the fame of Rhodes, its beauty and its roses as a sort of 'garden' in which Knights of Christ could rest after fighting God's foes. Meanwhile Pope Clement VI complained about Hospitaller extravagance. 'The administrators of the Order,' he said, 'ride great fine horses, feast on exquisite viands, wear magnificent apparel, drink from cups of gold and silver, and keep hawks and hounds for the chase.' Yet it would be wrong to accuse the Hospitallers of abandoning their deep if rather naive faith. The knights on Rhodes also cultivated a mystique of martyrdom, well illustrated in a speech by the papal legate before the sack of Alexandria in 1365. 'Chosen Knights of Christ,' he proclaimed, 'be comforted in the Lord and his Holy Cross. Fight manfully in God's war, fearing not your enemy and hoping for victory from God, for today the gates of Paradise are open.'

Religious relics played a significant role in such an atmosphere, the most important in Rhodes being an icon of the Virgin Mary, which was said to have been painted by the Apostle Luke himself. Following the siege of 1480 a church dedicated to Our Lady of Victory was built where the fighting had been fiercest. Eight years later, during a period of peace, the Ottoman Sultan Bayazid II gave the Order the right arm of John the Baptist and a thorn from Christ's crown, which had previously been in the Byzantine Imperial Treasury.

The fanaticism of the Hospitallers meant that they killed almost all male Muslim prisoners except for children, who were enslaved until a change of attitude in the mid-15th century, perhaps resulting from the Order's serious shortage of oarsmen for its galleys. The *servitudo marina* levy of Greek oarsmen was abandoned, and, instead, Turkish captives were used as galley slaves, along with the

An English carved misericorde representing the Fall of Pride and providing a fine illustration of the back of late 14th-century knightly armour. (*In situ*, Lincoln Cathedral, England)

19

buonavoglia volunteers who enlisted to pay off their debts. Many of the latter were Maltese even before the Order moved to that island. For their part the Turks did not usually kill Christian prisoners, and there are records of western European knights having experience of fighting in, rather than against, Ottoman armies. These would not, however, have included Hospitaller brethren.

The papacy had great influence over the Hospitaller Order during the 14th and 15th centuries. Hospitallers similarly became prominent figures within the papal court and papal states. Nevertheless, this close relationship meant that the Great Schism, with rival popes in Rome and Avignon, was a serious threat to Hospitaller unity. It is a tribute to the political skills of their leaders that the Order not only survived but played its part in ending the schism.

Despite the romantic ethos that grew up around Rhodes the Order's military activities in the 14th century were actually very limited, and much of the fighting was done by mercenaries in Hospitaller service. Much of this lack of action can be attributed to poor communication as well as inefficient administration, but it inevitably led to criticism. Some critics struck at the very purpose of the military orders, arguing that their belligerence was immoral, illegal and hindered the conversion of Muslims to Christianity. Other critics resented the way men of humble origin could rise to prominence within the Order and 'abuse' knights of nobler blood, while criticism of the Hospitallers' perceived wealth, power and pride was even more widespread.

Even the Pope himself contrasted the 'sloth' of the Hospitallers with the vigour of the Teutonic Knights. In 1352 the poet Petrarch wrote, 'Rhodes, Shield of the Faith, lies unwounded, inglorious,' and in the late 14th century Philip de Mézières claimed that brethren served four or five years in Rhodes simply to get a good preceptory or priory when they returned to Europe. Criticism from the Italian merchant republics was more worldly, with the Venetian Marino Sanudo accusing the Order of harbouring pirates because they had so few ships of their own. Accusations of protecting pirates became even fiercer in the 15th and early 16th centuries.

Within Europe Hospitaller brethren sometimes faced a clash of loyalties, since they still owed some loyalty to their native sovereigns. This was a particular problem in Spain and occasionally resulted in brethren being excommunicated by the Pope. Hospitallers could also find themselves caught between obedience to their *castellan* or preceptor, or his lieutenant or proctors, and the master, his lieutenants and others. In another and even more isolated region, Scandinavia, the

Hospitallers faced problems when local rulers confiscated a number of their properties. Perhaps it was partly in recognition of such difficulties that a new Hospitaller statute of 1367 allowed brethren to fight fellow Christians in defence of the Order, or of their secular lord, or for the common good.

Nor was Rhodes free from tensions between brethren. The worst case of internal violence came in 1381 when a Gascon Hospitaller, Fr Bertrin de Gagnac was suspected of involvement in the drowning of the drapier, the most senior Spanish brother on the island. In a resulting trial several women were tortured to confess that they had spread rumours. Eventually de Gagnac was accused of embezzling money, tried and condemned to lose his habit, but as the master tried to take the cloak de Gagnac struck at him with a dagger and was promptly cut down. A year later 56 brethren and donats were sent back to their European priories. In reality this was probably a disciplinary measure reflecting tensions between the French, Spaniards and others.

Hospitaller morale remained low throughout most of the 15th century and only improved with the successful defence of Rhodes against the Ottomans in 1480. Morale and prestige slumped again after the loss of Rhodes in 1522 and would only be regained with the successful defence of Malta 33 years later.

This early 16th-century wall painting by Pinturicchio is said to show Alberto Aringhierre as an idealistic young Hospitaller brother knight. As rector of the cathedral he donated the money to build this chapel. (*In situ*, Chapel of St John the Baptist, Cathedral, Siena, Italy)

COSTUME, ARMS AND ARMOUR

The 14th and 15th centuries were a period of major change in western European male costume. Loose clothes, which had much in common with Greek Orthodox, eastern European and Middle Eastern dress, were rapidly replaced by a distinctively western fashion for almost body-hugging male clothes. The Hospitallers, whose traditional robe-like garments reflected the Order's religious origins, were not immune from such changes, and many pictorial sources show that the brethren, when not actually involved in religious duties, wore clothes that differed little from those of the secular knightly class. Such distinctive western European fashions also helped the Hospitallers to make a clear visual distinction between themselves and Greek Orthodox Christians. Meanwhile the old prohibition against decorated weapons had virtually been abandoned. Pictorial sources illustrate sometimes magnificent decoration on both clothing, weaponry and horse-harnesses. Somehow Master de la Valette's ruling in 1558 that knights caught wearing embroidered stockings could face four years in the galleys does not sound entirely convincing as proof that Hospitaller brethren spurned worldly magnificence.

This period saw greater changes in western European armour than any other and the Hospitallers, who always attempted to have the best military equipment, naturally reflected such developments. Plate body

King Louis of France lands at Damietta in Egypt, in a French account illustrated around 1480. King Louis is accompanied by soldiers who wear red surcoats with white crosses, perhaps representing Hospitaller brethren. (*Livre des Faits de Monseigneur Saint Louis*, Bibliothèque Nationale, Ms. Fr. 2829, f.36v, Paris, France)

and limb protections of hardened leather and of iron had been known in Europe for a century or so, and their further adoption was not a regular process. Traditional and supposedly more advanced forms of armour co-existed at the same time and sometimes even in the same regions, while climatic factors played a part by apparently slowing the adoption of plate armour in hot areas like Italy, Spain, Latin Greece and the Balkans.

The armour, some of it far from new, which the Hospitallers abandoned at Rhodes in 1522, mostly consists of what would today be called munitions equipment. Very few of these items are of particularly high quality and they tend to destroy some romantic images of the medieval knight. Nor does it have the uniformity characteristic of medieval illustrations of armoured men. Instead the collection consists of a mixture of shapes, sizes and styles, some decorated but mostly plain, and almost none of it very shiny or new when being used.

The recycling of military equipment had been characteristic of the Hospitallers since the 12th century and continued at least until the 16th century. In April 1555, for example, a statute repeated that the weapons of deceased brethren should revert to the Order, but with interesting exceptions. Paragraph 24, volume D, stated:

This anonymous but thoughtful-looking young member of the Order was painted by Francesco Francia in the early 16th century. (National Gallery, London, England)

> *All arms of whatever description left by Knights deceased, either in Malta or abroad, become the property of the Treasury. They shall be kept in order so as to be available, in case of want, for the protection of our Convent [Malta]. Exception shall, however, be made in the case of swords and daggers which shall be sold by public auction.*

The Hospitallers were clearly enthusiastic when it came to the adoption of firearms, the Prior of Catalonia having a *bombarda* (or large cannon) as early as 1395. In 1531 the Order in Malta was eager to obtain good cannon whenever possible and in that year a ship arrived from England laden with guns as a gift from King Henry VIII. Apparently they ranged from large artillery pieces to small items including a surviving shield with a handgun in the centre.

Several descriptions of the process of arming a knight survive and although none of them relate specifically to a Hospitaller they are still relevant. The first comes from an English version of the story of *Sir Gawain and the Green Knight* dating from around 1370 (translated by Helmut Nickel):

> *Early he calls for his arms, and they all were brought. At first a red carpet was spread on the floor, and there was much gilded gear that gleamed piled upon it. The bold man steps on it and takes the steel in hand. He was arrayed in a doublet of rich fabric of Tarsia, and then a well-made capados, close-fitted, that was lined with light-coloured fur. Then they set the sabatons on the man's feet. His legs were enclosed in*

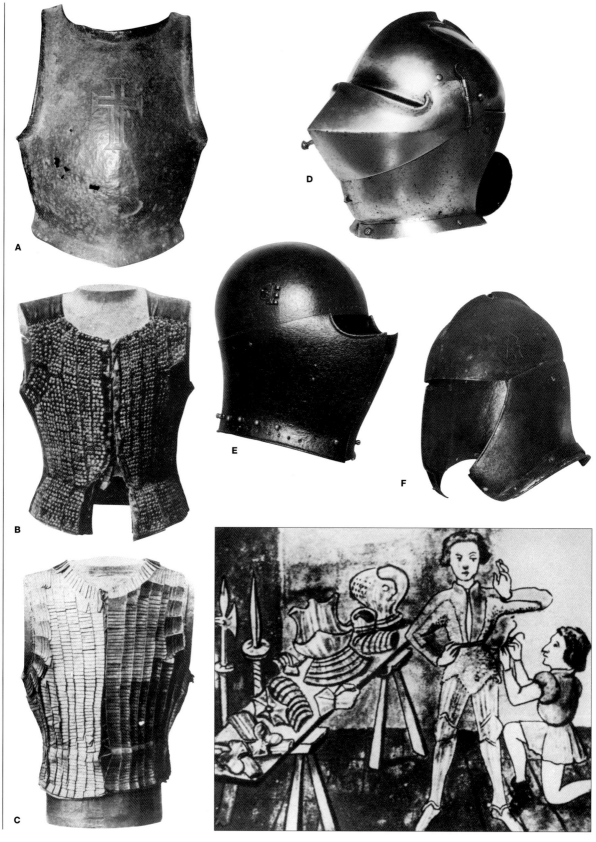

A

B

C

D

E

F

24

steel by elegant greaves with attached poleyns. Brightly polished, they were fastened around his knees with golden buckles. Then came the cuisses that snugly enclosed his brawny thighs, attached by means of straps. And afterwards the byrnie, wrought of bright steel rings, enveloped the rich fabric [of the doublet he already wore]. And they set well-burnished vambraces upon both his arms, with good and shiney couters and gauntlets of plate. And all the fine equipment that he needed this time, with splendid coat-armour, his golden spurs proudly fastened on, girt with a trusty sword with a silken belt to his side.

Just over 50 years later another English text, the *Worship of Arms* by Johan Hill the armourer to King Henry VI, described what a gentleman needed to fight in his sovereign's wars:

First him needeth to have a pair of hose of whipcorde without vampeys. And the said hose cut at the knees and lined within with linen cloth cut on the bias as the hose are. A pair of shoes of red leather laced and fretted underneath with whipcord & persed [given a thin leather sole]. *And above within lined with linen cloth three fingers broad, doubled and biased from the toe and anklebone to above the ankle. And so behind at the heel from the sole half a quarter of a yard from this so as to fasten well his sabatons. And the same sabatons fastened under the sole of the foot in two places. Him needeth also a petycote as an overbody of a doublet. His petycote without sleeves, the sizes of it three-quarters around without a collar and reaching no further than the waist and a doublet also with straight sleeves, collar, and certain eyelets on the sleeves for the vambraces and the rerebraces. Armed in this manner, first put on the sabatons, greaves and tight cuisses with voydours of plate or of mail and a close breech* [for the groin] *of mail with five steel buckles and fine leather straps. And all the arming points after they have been knit and fastened upon him, ensure that the points be cut off* [meaning the remaining lengths of leather lace be removed]. *And then a pair of close gussets* [of mail], *ensuring that the gussets extend three fingers' width within the edges of his plates* [cuirass] *on both sides. And then a pair of plates of 20 pounds weight on his breast, and these plates secured also with wire or with* [leather] *points. A pair of rerebraces from within the plates with two forelocks* [buckled straps] *in the front and three forelocks behind. A pair of vambraces closed with voydours of mail and fretted. A pair of gloves* [gauntlets] *in whatever style is suitable. A bascinet suited to the lists is not suitable for other battles, but when fighting man to man it is said 'necessity hath no law'. The bascinet locked with a bevor and visor which is locked or strapped also to the chest and back with two forelocks. And this aforesaid Gentleman, when he is thus armed and ready to come to the field, will have on him a coat-armour* [a tabard at this period] *of single cloth which is better when fighting. And his leg harness covered all over with red tarityn* [cloth], *the which has been called the tincturing of his leg armour because in this manner his opponent will not so easily see his blood. And therefore also his hose should be red for in all other colours the blood will easily be seen. During the olden times in such a battle nothing should have been seen except his helmet and his gauntlets. And finally tie upon him a pair of besagewes* [steel discs to protect the shoulder joints].

STRATEGY, TACTICS, TRAINING AND NAVAL WARFARE

The Mamluk defeat of the Mongols, followed by the conversion of the latter to Islam, effectively marked the end of crusader attempts to retake the Holy Land by using Cyprus as a naval base. Instead Cyprus served as a base from which to raid Islamic coasts and support the Christian mainland kingdom of Cilician Armenia. The Hospitallers contributed to both these strategies. The Order also favoured a series of limited campaigns against the Mamluks, for which the Hospitaller master proposed a force of 1,000 knights and 4,000 crossbowmen to serve for five years. They should be supported by 60 galleys, based in Rhodes, which were to operate for eight months each year. The master even suggested that overland trade routes to India be developed to divert trade away from Egypt and thus undermine the Mamluk sultanate's economy.

This sophisticated concept indicated how modern Hospitaller strategic thinking was, yet it remained beyond medieval western European capabilities. It was even impossible to impose a naval blockade on Egypt, which was five or six days sailing from Cyprus. Medieval fleets had to operate in fair summer weather, which meant that food and water

This little-known early 16th-century painted wood carving is believed to illustrate the martyrdom of St William. It also shows an unusual form of trousered mail hauberk with a laced mail flap that enabled the man to relieve himself. (*In situ*, Church of St Guillaume, Strasbourg, France)

deteriorated rapidly. It was similarly difficult to maintain the health of armies if they had to remain in one place too long. So, recognising reality, Hospitaller strategy shifted from the eastern Mediterranean to the Aegean, and in 1375 the Order proposed a crusade in support of the crusader states of Greece. It was to consist of 125 brethren from the French priories, 108 from the Italian, 73 from the Iberian, 38 from the English and Irish, 32 from the German and Bohemian, 17 from the Hungarian and two each from the preceptories of Morea and Athens, each with their squires. In the event the Order failed to assemble anywhere near this number and the proposal was a flop. Elsewhere there was little fighting on land against the Turks, except skirmishes that merely provoked the enemy and were stopped in 1409.

Meanwhile the Hospitaller fleet had evolved into an elite since the early 14th century, but because it was so small, consisting on average of only four war galleys, it could rarely conduct independent action. Instead the Order's ships were responsible for the maritime defence of Rhodes. After Izmir fell to Timur-i Lenk in 1402 the fleet was enlarged and turned its attention to the persistent raiding of Ottoman commerce, while the massive new castle at Bodrum gave the Hospitallers a new mainland outpost. This, and the Hospitaller-held offshore islands, enabled galleys to attack passing merchant ships almost at will.

ABOVE LEFT **Mail shirt made in Sinigaglia, 14th-century Italian. (private collection)**

ABOVE RIGHT **A composite armour consisting of items found in Rhodes and photographed early in the 20th century. The helmet has since been lost.**

The Hospitallers' victims, of course, saw this corsair warfare as mere piracy. So the Turks retaliated with annual raids on Rhodes or the other islands, seeking to undermine the Hospitaller economy by cutting down orchards or vineyards, burning farm buildings, and seizing livestock and captives who were resettled on the mainland. This in turn obliged the Hospitallers to erect many small towers as refuges for the local people and herds. The Hospitaller master also had spies in the main Ottoman naval base of Gallipoli, and there was usually a Hospitaller patrol boat in the vicinity that would race back to Rhodes with a warning if the Ottoman fleet emerged. When a major Turkish assault came in 1480, the Ottoman sultan only sent part of his army because he was also campaigning on other fronts. Nevertheless, the Hospitaller galleys did not intercept the enemy at sea but were instead held back, perhaps to maintain communications with the outside world.

The Order's greatest naval success in the early 16th century was the destruction of a Mamluk fleet in the Gulf of Iskenderun in 1510. It may, however, have been a strategic disaster, for this apparently unprovoked attack destroyed good relations between the Hospitallers and the Mamluks, and seven years later the Mamluk sultanate was conquered by the Ottomans. Henceforth the Hospitallers were alone except for the Venetians, whose policy was to maintain peace with the Ottoman Empire, and the Genoese, who clung to some islands north of Hospitaller territory. The continued existence of an aggressive crusader outpost straddling the sea route from Istanbul to the Ottomans' new

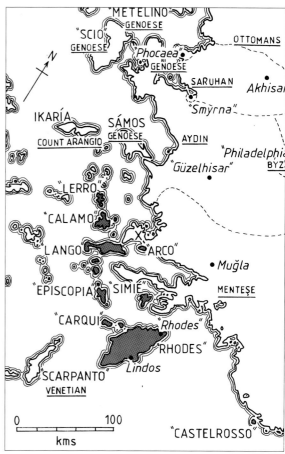

province of Egypt was, however, intolerable for the Turkish sultan, and when the crisis came in 1522 the Turks moved so fast that Rhodes fell with relative ease.

This was a period that saw a great deal of theoretical military writing, most of which was intended for leaders. There was also a 'gentlemanly' way of fighting in which skill with weapons and the use of armour were the marks of a knight. This involved agility, the striking and evading of blows, parrying and speed of reactions, as well as hard training and a recognition that excessively heavy armour or closed helmets could cause exhaustion. In fact the Greek climate and the conditions of close combat aboard a warship may account for the widespread preference for open-faced helmets such as bascinets and salets.

The use of large amounts of plate armour declined in the 16th century, largely as a result of more effective firearms. Before that happened, however, the late medieval swordsman faced a variety of efficient forms of body armour, not always of plate. The initial result was the development of heavier and more pointed sword blades. Greater emphasis was also given to the *foyne* or thrust. For example, a unique late 13th-century Latin text on fencing written in Germany shows many complex cuts and thrusts to shins and feet, as well as sword parries and counter-strikes with a small shield. The first known treatise dealing with a new Italian style of fencing that relied on a single longsword, was the *Flos Duellatorium* by Fiore dei Liberi, written in 1410. Other 15th-century

Italian and German works describe the use of infantry weapons, and there was even a book on wrestling by Otto the Jew.

Paradoxically, some of the best accounts of Hospitaller warfare are found in Turkish. For example, the *Destan of Umur Pasha*, written in the mid-15th century, described how the Order and other crusaders attacked a Turkish position outside Izmir:

> *In the morning the enemy put on their cuirasses and arms. Their horse-armour, their cuirasses were amazing. Their gauntlets, their arm-defences, their leg defences, their helmets, all shone and twinkled in the light. Those who carried small crossbows came in front, those who carried large crossbows and arrows followed. There were an infinite number carrying javelins and shields, and as numerous were those with swords and daggers. … They surged up from the sea and made their assault. In the wink of an eye they reached the ditch. They carried fire to burn the mangonels. They wielded very long axes and broke all the palisades in the ditch.*

The failed Mamluk siege of Rhodes in 1444 is said to have been the model for sieges in *Tirant lo Blanc* by Martorell. The author described how soldiers slept in their armour so as to be ready for battle early the following morning, and wielded battleaxes as the most effective weapon against heavily armoured opponents. Countermines beneath the walls were supposedly filled with brass bowls that rattled if enemy miners were working nearby. Pans filled with chopped goats' hair and mutton fat were lit at midnight, causing foul-smelling smoke to stampede the besiegers' cattle. Concern for livestock was clearly a feature of Hospitaller Rhodes. During the first Ottoman siege of 1480 the turcopolier and his men were responsible for gathering such animals and available supplies of grain into the safety of the city. This turcopolier was also in charge of coastal defence, observation and signalling.

Hospitaller naval warfare, as described by men who returned to Spain, may have been the model for naval battles in *Tirant lo Blanc*. War

 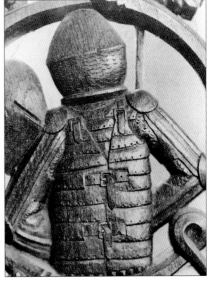

Wood carving of an armoured knight made *c.*1360–1370, showing the front and back. His German armour is of a type that would have been used by Hospitaller brethren based within the Empire. (*In situ*, Levitic Pew, Verden Cathedral, Germany)

galleys changed from the late 13th to mid-14th centuries – the old system whereby one oarsman pulled one oar being replaced by a system whereby five to seven oarsmen pulled a single large oar. By the late 15th century it was traditional for Hospitaller galleys to be larger than those of other fleets, except Venice, which enabled them to keep the seas for a longer period and in worse weather – sometimes even through winter.

Rhodes had sufficient timber to repair but not construct many ships, most of which were built in Genoa or Marseilles. Even so, the Order had materials sent to Rhodes. In the late 15th century, for example, the master ordered the commander of Savona in Italy to send two galleys and their crews, plus '400 pieces of cotton cloth, 200 for sails for galleys and 200 for [merchant] ships, 300 oars, and ropes and hawsers for two galleys.' It was normal for Aegean galleys to be taken out of the water during winter, and this was probably also true in the Rhodes arsenal or *tersenal*. Otherwise galleys were moored in the main harbour, not in the neighbouring Mandraccio cove as was once thought.

The Hospitaller admiral was in charge of all the Order's galleys and of any other ordinary ships that were armed for war. He could also hire additional galleys, but even the admiral and, of course, the fighting men aboard ship were under the command of the marshal if he was present. Following a landing, the knights were placed under the commander of knights.

Little information seems to survive concerning the armaments aboard Hospitaller ships, but this is likely to have been much the same as that aboard other galleys. For example, Venetian galleys in the 14th-century Aegean carried 30 to 50 men armed with swords and 10 to 20 with crossbows. Other regulations stipulated the type of armour to be carried. Genoese naval regulations of around 1330, which are likely to have been similar to Hospitaller practice, stipulated that a galley with a

The English tower at one corner of the powerful Hospitaller castle of St Peter in Bodrum, on the Aegean coast of Turkey. (Photograph Mary Orr)

crew of 176 men include junior officers and 12 crossbowmen, four of whom were considered specialists with two weapons each. The ship was also 'armed' with 160 cuirasses, 160 gorgets, 170 helmets, 12 other crossbows, 5,000 crossbow bolts, plus spears, javelins and bills. The ship's captain and the ship's scribe were expected to have heavier armour than the others, while the *nauclerius* or sailing master had rather less. By 1483 the weaponry aboard a pilgrim galley also included cannon. In galleys the forecastle formed the focus of both defence and attack, this being where most armoured men were stationed.

Service aboard ship was called *carovane* and was obligatory for all Hospitaller brethren. Here they would find themselves in command of very motley crews, since the pool of sailors, oarsmen and naval troops in the Aegean region included Russians, Italians, Greeks, Spaniards and assorted peoples from the Black Sea coast. Naval tactics were based on raiding enemy coasts and ambushing merchant ships, the small *galiote* with 12 to 22 rowing benches being best for raiding. Good local knowledge was one reason for the success of Hospitaller galleys and this was obviously necessary when, as was usually the case, two galleys worked together. One would lie in wait behind a headland or small island, while the second harried a victim into the jaws of this ambush. When the Hospitallers did meet the enemy at sea they would use boarding tactics, usually relying on the raised *calcar* or 'beak' that was a feature of medieval Mediterranean galleys.

ABOVE LEFT **The grand master giving orders during the Ottoman siege of Rhodes in 1480. (*Obsidionis Rhodie Urbis Descriptio*, Bibliothèque Nationale, Ms. Lat. 6067, f.33v, Paris, France)**

ABOVE RIGHT **A printed version of Guillaume Caoursin's account of the siege of 1480 was published within 20 years of the event and was illustrated with woodcuts.**

Coastal raids could involve larger forces. *Tirant lo Blanc* again offers a vivid picture, with a flotilla of galleys approaching in close formation so that they all hit the beach at the same time. Even so they had to turn and backwater as the raiding party would disembark from the stern. The *Destan of Umur Pasha*, written in Turkish around the same time as *Tirant lo Blanc*, described such a descent on Izmir harbour by Hospitallers and others: 'Thirty galleys were sent to Izmir, all filled with men in full armour. … These innumerable Franks were dressed in iron from head to foot.' In a later verse the Turkish poet described the sound of the handguns or *tüfeks* in battle: 'shat! shat!'

Battles between fleets at sea were rare but when they did occur, galleys normally formed a loose line with larger transport galleys and sailing ships in reserve, while small vessels carried messages from ship to ship. A disparity between the sizes, numbers and tactics of Christian and Islamic warships is again reflected in *Tirant lo Blanc*. This refers to netting suspended over the decks to protect against heavy objects being dropped on a ship and, of course, to inhibit boarding. The waist and forecastle of a ship was also padded with available mattresses against early cannon. Armour was taken from the wounded during battle to be used by others, and after a victory the enemy dead and wounded were tipped into the sea. The size of Christian ships clearly impressed the Turkish author of the *Destan of Umur Pasha* who wrote that, 'their topsails are like fortresses. The cogs carry enemies without number.' Of course the 15th-century Turkish use of the term *cog* applied to a more sophisticated ship than the northern European cog from which it was taken. It may, in fact, have referred to the great carracks that the Hospitallers used in combination with their already large galleys from the late 15th century onwards.

The Hospitallers' biggest and most ambitious great carrack was laid down at Nice the same year that the Order lost Rhodes. It was the *Santa Anna* which, launched in 1524, became the most powerful fighting vessel in the Mediterranean. She had four masts, 3,000 tonnes displacement, the first metal-sheathed bottom known in Europe, two gun decks, 50 large cannon and many smaller, an armoury for 500 soldiers and 100 brother knights, and provisions for six months at sea. In addition to one large bakery and other stoves, the *Santa Anna* carried a grove of cypress trees and some mandarin orange trees as a floating palace for the master and his court.

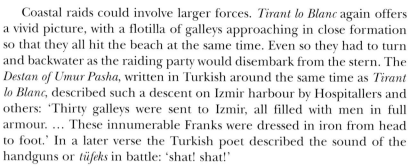

The most authoritative illustrations of 16th-century naval warfare in the Aegean come from Italian rather than Hospitaller sources. Here a squadron of Venetian galleys forms a line of battle, supported by six other galleys, in a manuscript made in 1553–1554 (*Trattato della Militia Maritima*, location unknown)

War at sea, mid-14th century

A

Brother knight-in-arms c.1330

A preceptor touring his estate, c.1375

c

Brother knight, c.1430

The Hospitallers defend Rhodes from the Mamluk fleet, 1444

E

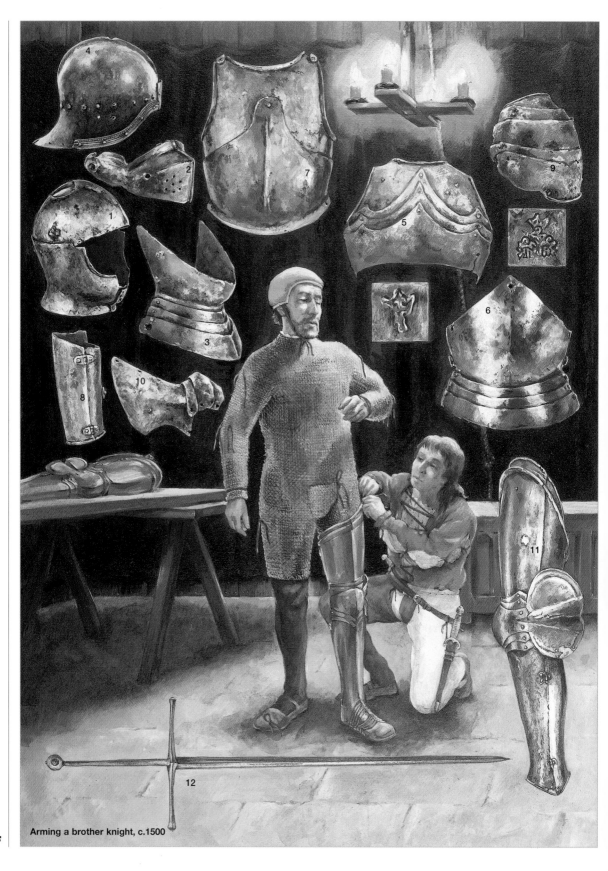

F

Arming a brother knight, c.1500

Heraldry of the masters 1306–1565, and a brother knight in full ceremonial dress c.1525

1

2

3

4

5

6a

6b

7

8

9

10

11

12

13

14

15

16

17

18

19

20

21

22

23

24

G

H

Investiture of two novitiates as full brethren of the Order, mid-16th century

SUPPORT SERVICES

Maintaining a military outpost far from their western European powerbase and in an increasingly hostile part of the world required efficient support mechanisms. Given the limited technology and administrative systems available, those of the Hospitallers were remarkably effective. At the same time Rhodes served as an important centre for peaceful trade within the Aegean and as a safe harbour on the long journey to and from the Middle East. Nor would it seem that shipwreck was inevitably disastrous. There are numerous references to ships and galleys being wrecked in the Aegean, yet their passengers and crews continued their journeys in the next available ship. Larger ships were clearly safer and could keep sailing in worse weather. The Hospitaller vessel *Mont Joye*, for example, ran a regular service from Marseilles in southern France to Famagusta in Cyprus between 1300 and 1314. Sometimes these vessels operated with remarkably small crews, and it has been suggested that new shipboard technologies reduced the need for large crews in the 14th century. Nevertheless the danger from pirates usually resulted in an increased number of crossbowmen and marines in dangerous waters.

Some of the Hospitallers' Aegean islands were quite fertile, particularly Lango (Kos), while food could also be brought from the Order's nearby estates in Cyprus. Yet such supplies were limited and large amounts of foodstuffs were regularly shipped from western Europe to Rhodes. In fact the famous windmills that lined the Rhodes harbour mole ground the grain, most of which came from Sicily. Little is known about the diet of the brethren stationed in the Aegean, but those at Villel in Aragon dined on a healthy diet of beef, eels, chicken and wine.

Rhodes needed to import horses and other pack animals which, in time of peace, could be purchased on the Turkish mainland. There was also a trade in animals between the Greek islands. On the other hand, horses were now less important to the Order than they had been in the Middle East, except, of course, in Iberia where the Hospitallers of Aragon had their own studs at Miravet, Alfambra and elsewhere.

Despite its wealth the Order continued to re-use military equipment, and this was still reflected in the judgements of the central chapter during the 14th century. War horses, saddle horses, mules, saddles, horse harnesses, bridles and head stalls still reverted to the master, as did plate armour, breastplates, plackarts, leather cuirasses, mail hauberks, helmets, chapels-de-fer, banners, pennants, swords,

One of the functions of the Hospitaller castle at Kolossi in Cyprus was to protect an important sugar-processing plant next door.
(Photograph A. F. Kersting)

Though considerably restored, this mid-14th-century wall painting offers a detailed picture of the sort of saddle and harness that would have been used by Hospitaller brethren. (*In situ*, Cathedral, Bergamo; author's photograph)

Turkish arms, javelins, lances, horse armour, crossbows, longbows and crowbars for sieges. Clothing and bedding went to the drapier or the master, though some went to the hospitaller, infirmarian, grand commander or conventual prior. The items mentioned in such judgements similarly suggested that brethren now lived in some luxury, with silk bedspreads, blankets, sheets, cushions, pillows, curtains, mattresses, wall hangings, carpets, Turkish carpets, rugs, livery or heraldic rugs, mats, leather buckrams, assorted cloth including gold cloth, samite, sendal, silk and wool, plus kerchiefs, table napkins, towels new and used, plain and embroidered *berettas*, brimmed hats, cassocks, and belts both plain and woven. Table or kitchen items went to the master or grand commander, including silver goblets with and without feet, drinking 'tubes', gold and silver plate, table knives, silver spoons, basins, kitchen utensils, drawers and wine. Books and liturgical items reverted to the master, grand commander or conventual prior, including breviaries, chapelles, missals, psalters, Roman psalters which seem to have been special, silver cups and holy water vessels. Miscellaneous items allocated to the master, grand commander or drapier included amber, money belts, rings, wallets, boxes, chests, coffers and soap. Hospitaller life was not one of penance and poverty.

As the Hospitallers became wealthier they, like ordinary monastic orders, needed legal advice to guard their interests. They could hire lawyers, but this was expensive, and hired men might not be wholly committed to the Hospitaller cause. Or the Hospitallers could attract legally trained men into the Order, but in this they were not very successful. So the Order started training some of its own brethren as lawyers. Some Hospitaller houses in Paris, near the Schools of Canon Law, became hostels, and from 1380 onwards an informal Hospitaller *studium* or college of canon law operated in the city. From the late 14th century it was standard practice for at least one of the Hospitaller's proctor generals not only to be a fully trained lawyer but also to be a brother of the Order.

EVERYDAY LIFE AND CULTURE

After the Hospitallers conquered Rhodes they enlarged the Byzantine governor's palace and converted the walled city into their *collachio* or segregated area, while the Greek population was expelled to a new suburb. At the top of the main street of the collachio was an open square flanked by the palace of the master and the main church of St John. At the bottom of the main street stood the cathedral, the arsenal and a gate through the harbour wall to the inner harbour. Both sides of the street were lined with conventual buildings, many being the headquarters of various langues. Brethren no longer lived in one big auberge, as had been traditional in the Holy Land, but had separated into auberges for each langue while in Cyprus. In Rhodes most brethren probably did not actually live in the communal auberge, which may have been used by men recently arrived or on short visits. The rest probably lived in smaller houses within the collachio though the auberge remained the centre of their communal and religious life.

The collachio and the neighbouring fortified suburb were clearly impressive, as described by an anonymous English visitor in 1345:

> *Within the castle walls are an archbishop and his metropolitan church, and the dwellings of the many citizens are like those of distinguished men. There are moneyers, armourers, and all the artificers necessary to a city or a royal castle. Below the castle is the house of the hospital* [the infirmary], *with a mother-nurse, doctor, protector, and handmaiden to all the infirm.*

A great many languages were spoken in this bustling city, not only among the brethren but also by local inhabitants and merchants. Another visitor to Rhodes in 1521 said there were so many languages that each corrupted the other and none were spoken properly. Many brethren would have learned a little conversational Greek, but a few studied the language and translated classical texts. Greek was used in diplomatic exchanges between the Order and the Turkish states, since there seems to have been virtually no understanding of Turkish, though some Arabic was also used for diplomatic or commercial purposes.

Despite occasional lapses, relations between the Hospitallers and the Mamluk sultanate became quite good from the late 14th to early 16th centuries. In 1403 an official treaty strengthened this relationship, under which the Hospitallers assumed the role of protectors of Christian holy places in Palestine. Both sides agreed to give three months' notice of warlike activity, but

The 14th-century basement beneath the manor house at Hether in Leicestershire. The building was once a Hospitaller commandery. (Photograph Mrs. P. Hodge)

this amicable arrangement was constantly disturbed by Christian pirates based in the Hospitaller islands. The Order was also permitted to keep a consul in the Egyptian port of Damietta to ransom captives and buy duty-free food. The Hospitallers had their own prisoners, especially after the Order gave up its traditional habit of slaughtering male Muslim captives. Many of these prisoners were used in the galleys, but some may have been kept as bargaining chips. The Ottoman Prince Cem obviously fell into this category and his comfortable exile in a Hospitaller house in France allowed him to indulge in at least one scandalous love affair with the daughter of a guard. It may also have been true of captured Ottoman officers, such as the senior man and 12 others who eluded their guards in Rhodes and tried to swim to a Spanish ship in 1504.

Back in western Europe life for most Hospitallers was probably one of humdrum routine, supervising an agricultural estate. The relationship between presbyters or commanders and their peasantry seems generally to have been good, and there were cases where a newly arrived commander had to swear to protect his villagers before they would swear fealty to him. Sometimes the resulting vassalage was symbolised by a shared meal which might be in the commander's residence or in the peasant's own house.

St John the Evangelist on Patmos in an early 15th-century French manuscript sent with other gifts to the Hospitaller convent in Rhodes.
(*The Rhodes Missal*, Library and Museum of the Order of St John, London, England)

Elsewhere a commander imposed the Order's domination by controlling the local baking oven and refusing to allow the construction of another. Instead villagers had to give the Order one loaf in every 20 in return for the use of this solitary oven.

Providing hospitality to travellers and pilgrims now formed a small aspect of Hospitaller duties and Hospitaller hospices were largely superseded by ordinary inns in the rapidly expanding cities. Meanwhile the number of pilgrims making the long journey to the Holy Land declined in the 15th century, and the larger ships no longer necessarily stopped at Rhodes on their way.

The Hospitallers' medical duties similarly declined in importance and the Order's infirmaries may largely have been superseded by *maisons-dieu* run by secular urban authorities. Yet the main infirmary in Rhodes was too important a symbol of the Order's original charitable function to be left to decay. In fact the Hospitallers had a functioning infirmary in Rhodes as early as 1311. This was rebuilt by Master Roger de Pins and remained in use until 1483 when an entirely new infirmary was ready to accept patients. The building, greatly restored by the Italians during the First World War, is the best preserved of the Order's conventual infirmaries. The pilier or leader of the French langue was the hospitaller in charge of this infirmary, though the infirmarian, a sergeant from the French langue, actually ran it. He visited the sick and supervised medical treatment, while his scribe recorded medical details and wrote down wills. Two *probi homines* or *prodomi* ('proven men') looked after the infirmary's supplies and kept accounts while a chaplain supervised its religious life and administered the sacraments. A pharmacy was also established along with a system to check the quality of drugs and medicaments. Two doctors and two surgeons actually treated the patients, visiting them every evening and morning on penalty of a fine. Most physicians in Rhodes were salaried laymen, mostly Italians or Jews, but all brother knights had to do nursing duties at some time, and even the masters washed bedridden patients.

The new infirmary was itself two storeys high, built around two courtyards. The east side of the first storey consisted of a hall used as the main ward. There were also some single rooms, probably for high officers and visiting nobles. Another large room was probably the refectory, next to a kitchen. A series of small cubicles down one side of the great wall are believed to have been properly ventilated privies, though the central one, immediately above the main entrance, was the infirmary chapel. In earlier Hospitaller infirmaries such privies had been located outside the main building. The ground floor consisted mainly of service rooms, but its east side was divided into eight bays that opened on to the street. The central one was the entrance, but the others seem to have been shops, rented out to provide an income for the resident clergy. There may also have been a surgery on the ground floor, along with other service and storage areas. This was probably for reasons of hygiene, though it would have kept noises and screaming at a distance. A smaller courtyard bordered the infirmary's vegetable and medicinal herb gardens.

The similarity between the layout of this new infirmary and various examples of Islamic architecture has long been recognised, but to draw parallels with the famous *khans* or roadside inns in Turkey is probably less valid than to draw them between this Rhodes infirmary and earlier *maristan* hospitals in Syria.

After 1403 good relations with the Mamluk sultanate enabled the Hospitallers to revive their first infirmary in Jerusalem and to have a consul in Ramla to assist pilgrims. Brethren assigned to this infirmary

The effigy of Ulrich de Huss dates from 1345 to 1350. The armour is typical of the German empire and includes plated vambraces to protect the lower arms. Rhodes received arms and armour from most parts of western Europe, including Germany. (Musée Unterlinden, Colmar, France)

were permitted to improve its buildings as well as repair the fabric of the Church of the Holy Sepulchre and some other Christian sites. Furthermore they were allowed to cross Mamluk territory on horseback, a great privilege in Mamluk society.

After losing Rhodes, the Hospitallers established a temporary infirmary at Messina in Sicily, and at their temporary headquarters in Viterbo on the Italian mainland. The Order then moved to Malta, but instead of immediately attempting to recreate the lost infirmary of Rhodes, they demolished some houses in Birgu to build a simple new ward for injured brethren. More rooms were added in 1538, but this infirmary proved inadequate during the great siege of 1565 when several houses had to be taken over as wards for the wounded.

The general level of culture within the Order increased from the 14th to the 16th centuries but was not evenly spread. Even in the 14th century the widespread illiteracy of recruits hindered their instruction. Among the Hospitaller elite there were, however, several highly educated men. Master Juan Fernandez de Heredia, for example, helped make the papal court at Avignon the centre of European culture for a while, building a big library, encouraging scholarship, meeting Greek scholars from the east and forging links with famous early Renaissance figures in Florence.

Rhodes itself became an early centre of Greek studies and among those scholars attracted to Rhodes was an Englishman named William Lily, the first headmaster of St Paul's School in London. Nevertheless the classical interests of some Hospitallers in Rhodes attracted accusations of idolatry or heresy from other brethren and they themselves sometimes complained that military duties interrupted their studies. One of the most interesting Hospitaller 'classicists' was Fr Sabba da Castiglione who visited archaeological sites and studied classical statues. He acted as a local agent for the noble Isabella Gonzaga, purchasing antique fragments and statues which he shipped back to Italy.

Meanwhile there remained a strange unwillingness for the Hospitallers to publicise their Order's achievements or to counter widespread criticism. The first general history of the Hospitallers seems to have been written by Fr Melchiore Bandini, the procurator and chancellor, in the 1440s. Some of the writing on Rhodes was less esoteric. For example, a late 15th-century brother knight, Fr Jean de Fransières who later became Prior of Aquitaine, wrote a book on falconry, and it is clear that the Hospitallers played a significant role in spreading Islamic knowledge on this and veterinary science to Europe. Another literary figure was Fr Laudivio Zacchia. The master agreed that the Order would finance his studies in Bologna University for four years after which he should return to Rhodes. Later Fr Zacchia became a famous poet and philosopher. It is also worth noting that Guillaume Caoursin, the master's secretary who wrote a famous account of the Ottoman siege of Rhodes in 1480, was not himself a brother of the Order. His book, the *Obsidionis Rhodie Urbis Descriptio*, was nevertheless so popular that a printed version was published within four months of the siege.

A woodcut print showing Hospitaller brethren, servants and physicians visiting the sick, dating from 1493.

Hospitaller scholars of the 16th century included even more exotic individuals. Fr Jean Quiton was born in Autun in 1500, travelled around the eastern Mediterranean, joined the Hospitallers, served in the master's household and was part of the commission that studied Malta before the Order agreed to move there. He subsequently became Professor of Canon Law at Paris University. Fr Antonio Pigafetta accompanied Magellan on his first circumnavigation of the world, then dedicated his account of this epic voyage to the master of the Order in 1524. In 1542 and 1553 Fr Nicholas Durand de Villegaignon wrote accounts of recent north African campaigns in which he himself took part. Later he became a Protestant and attempted to colonise Brazil. The Hospitaller Fr Antoine de Geoffroi travelled widely in the Near and Middle East, then published a book about Islam and the Ottoman empire which contained the Lord's Prayer in Turkish. Perhaps he was aware that this prayer from a person who Muslims recognise as the 'Prophet Jesus' is the only Christian prayer that some Islamic schools of law permit a Muslim to recite. De Geoffroi's book was certainly very objective, given the highly charged period in which he lived. Fr Antoine de Geoffroi was later accepted into the English langue, became lieutenant to the turcopolier in 1555 and ended his Hospitaller career as the senior man in the Scottish preceptory of Torphichen.

RIGHT **The infirmary in Rhodes during the 15th century (after Hattersley-Smith).**
A **Ground floor**
   X – underground passage
   S – shops opening to the street
   CC – central courtyard.
B **First floor**
   H – infirmary hall
   P – privies
   C – chapel over the main entrance
   R – single rooms
   F – refectory.
C **The hospital at Magione in Umbria as it probably appeared during the later 12th century (after Pardi).**
D **The Hospitaller-fortified hospital at Magione with 14th century additions (after Pardi).**

BELOW **The 15th-century Hospitaller infirmary in Rhodes, showing the shops that would have been rented out for income on the ground floor. (Photograph Greek Tourist Department)**

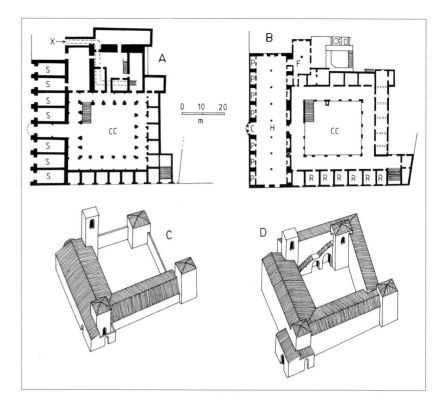

FORTIFICATION AND SIEGES

The Hospitaller defences of Rhodes and Bodrum were far more impressive than most other Latin crusader, Venetian and Genoese fortifications in the Aegean. The latter tended to be small, old fashioned and often of poor quality. The Venetians only started to erect more impressive fortresses in later years. Similarly late medieval Byzantine fortifications, with the notable exception of Constantinople (Istanbul), were relatively simple, while the Turks erected few castles at all.

In contrast to these humble rivals, the Hospitaller city of Rhodes became one of the strongest fortified positions in the Mediterranean. The Order started, in fact, with a rather weak location dominated by a nearby hill. To compensate for what was in effect a reverse slope, the Hospitallers dug a deep ditch in front of Rhodes' land wall, ten metres deep and 17 wide. Most of the 14th-century main wall had a *fausse-braie* or lower wall in front, while the curtain wall itself had a series of rectangular towers. Several of these stood separately in front of the wall, being linked to it by stone bridges. Some scholars regard these separate towers as a Hospitaller invention in response to the threat from cannonfire. In reality they were invented in 12th- and 13th-century Islamic north Africa and Andalusia. The idea was then presumably brought to Rhodes by Spanish brethren. As in Iberia, such isolated towers could resist as independent mini-forts even if the curtain wall fell to the enemy. Nor would their collapse necessarily cause a breach in that wall. The sea-walls of the city of Rhodes were largely built during the mastership of Fr Dieudonné de Gozon in the mid-14th century. The 15th century saw various projects to strengthen Rhodes' defences still further, the Tower of Master de Naillac being erected at the entrance to

A   A late 15th-century Italian cinquedea short broadsword. (Private collection)

B   The hilt of an Italian sword dating from around 1440. (Private collection)

C   The hilt of a typical Iberian sword from the early 16th century. (Private collection)

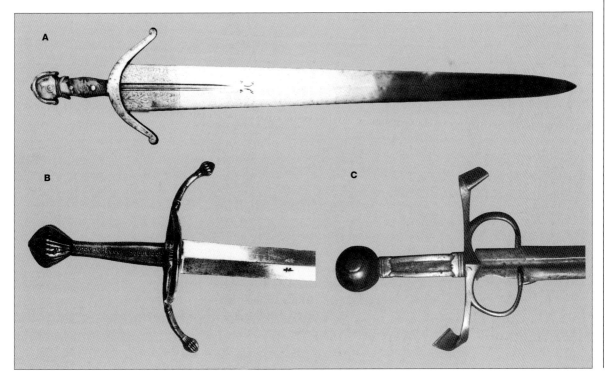

the harbour. The harbour entrance could also be closed by an iron chain, presumably supported on wooden floats as in Istanbul. It ran from the Tower of de Naillac to that of France, which stood at the end of the mole. A much larger and stronger Tower of St Nicholas was intended to close a gap in the defences shown during the Mamluk siege of 1444. It was again designed to resist in isolation and had walls eight metres thick.

Recent studies suggest that work on these 15th-century fortifications was mostly carried out by Rhodian Greek masons, the *magistri muratores* or 'master wall builders', who were exempt from other military service. They were recorded as working under the supervision of Jean Morelli, the prior of the main church. Three other Hospitaller brethren were also assigned to these building projects, though their precise role is unknown. Another effort to strengthen the walls after the Ottoman siege of 1480 was almost immediately outdated by rapid developments in cannon. So the master invited the most skilled Italian military architects to carry out a major updating. Italians were at this time leaders in military architecture and the famous Fabrizio del Carretto, who supervised the new works, had already worked for Emperor Maximilian. Meanwhile improvements were carried out to strategic fortresses at Bodrum and on the island of Lango (Kos).

All Hospitaller islands had castles of one kind or another and were also dotted with smaller towers to provide refuge in case of Turkish raids. Some castles overlooked major economic assets such as the saltpans on Castellorizo, which offered security not only to the workers but to their valuable salt. Castellorizzo was, however, too distant to form part of the remarkable chain of warning beacons that stretched from Leros in the north, via Bodrum, to Apolakia in southern Rhodes.

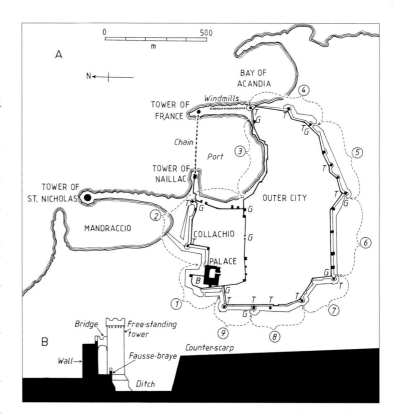

A **Fortifications of the city of Rhodes in 1480 (after Sire)**
G – gate
B – main bastion
T – free-standing tower.
Sections of wall defended by the master's household and each langue of the Order:
1 – Master's household
2 – France
3 – Castile
4 – Italy
5 – Provence
6 – Aragon
7 – England
8 – Auvergne
9 – Germany

B **Section through the land-walls in 1480, showing one of the free-standing towers.**

THE MOVE TO MALTA

The Hospitallers finally left Rhodes on 1 January 1523, after which the master sailed via Crete and Sicily to the papal states of central Italy. Most of the Greek Orthodox population remained and transferred their allegiance to the Ottoman sultan but some of the westernised Rhodian Greek elite chose to follow the Order into exile, eventually accompanying them to Malta.

Once settled in Italy the Hospitaller master was appointed guardian of the papal conclave that elected a new Pope in 1523. This Clement VII was a knight of the Order and had formerly been prior of Capua. For nearly four years the Hospitallers had their new headquarters in Viterbo, though they moved to Nice during an outbreak of plague in 1527. This was a period of great uncertainly for the Order, which found itself on the fringes of a prolonged war between France and Spain as well as being uncomfortably close to Rome when it was sacked. Pope Clement VII tried to make the Hospitallers into a tame papal guard.

Though the Order was in danger of falling apart, a series of important chapters general did what they could to sort out numerous problems concerning finances, administration and religious quarrels. Venetian hostility and the Lutheran Reformation were, in fact, greater threats to the Hospitallers' existence than Ottoman expansion. While the Venetian republic wanted peaceful relations with the Ottoman empire, the Hospitallers clung to their ancient ideology of permanent crusade. This they continued by privateering naval warfare that was intended to keep the eastern Mediterranean and Aegean seas as a permanent war zone. Meanwhile Venetian toleration of non-Christians within Venetian territory also shocked the Hospitallers.

The eight years between the fall of Rhodes and the acquisition of Malta saw the Order without a permanent home. Recruitment slumped, Hospitaller properties in England and Scandinavia were lost as a result of the Protestant Reformation and the English langue ceased to exist, except on paper. Elsewhere commanderies were raided by revolutionary Anabaptists, and even within Catholic Savoy and Portugal some properties were confiscated by local rulers. In Germany the situation was even more complicated. A few of the Order's own priests converted to Lutheranism and the number of German brother knights fell from 40 to 26. Some princes, including the powerful Margrave of Brandenburg, became Protestants and took over the Order's estates. In 1551 the Order finally declared the brethren in Brandenburg to be rebels. Nevertheless many other German brethren wanted a peaceful solution and this was eventually achieved at the end of the 16th century.

A painted wooden 'sepulchre', probably dating from the mid-15th century, showing typical central European armour of this period. (*In situ*, Cathedral, Erfurt, Germany; author's photograph)

By then the Hospitaller convent or headquarters was settled in its new home on Malta. After the fall of Rhodes, King Charles V of Spain had become the Order's most important patron and offered the Hospitallers both Malta and the vulnerable Spanish-ruled port of Tripoli in Libya. The French, who were then bitter rivals of Spain, resisted this handover, fearing that the Hospitallers would become an addition to Spanish military power. Nor were the Hospitallers particularly enthusiastic. The Order sent commissioners to look at alternatives, including Minorca, Ibiza and Ischia, but none were available, so the Hospitallers accepted what was on offer and moved to Malta in 1530.

Their commissioners' reports back, however, were not favourable. Wood was so scarce that it was sold by weight, cowdung and thistles were used as fuel and Malta did not lie on any important shipping lane. It was, however, an important centre of cotton production for making ships' sails, as well as a producer of the spice cumin. Some wheat and grapes were grown, but even without the presence of the Hospitallers, Malta had to import food. Neighbouring Gozo was more fertile but had no harbours, only 5,000 inhabitants and one weak castle. Many houses in Malta's main town of Mdina (Italian: Città Notabile) were derelict, while the small castle of Sant'Angelo, which defended a magnificent harbour on the east coast, had only three cannon and a few mortars. On the other hand this great harbour of Birgu (Italian: Il Borgo) was the best in the central Mediterranean after those of Syracuse and Taranto. The population of Malta consisted of about 12,000 Arabic-speaking peasants under a local aristocracy descended from Norman, Italian and Catalan conquerors. This Maltese nobility was not, in fact, keen on their island being handed over to the overbearing Hospitaller brethren, but they could do nothing about it.

In return for their new home, the Hospitallers agreed to pay an annual 'rent' of one hawk or gerfalcon to the King of Spain. They were also permitted to import Sicilian wheat free of duty. The Hospitallers selected the fishing town of Birgu rather than Mdina as their headquarters, and promptly set about strengthening the fort of Sant'Angelo. Birgu grew slowly and, after the Order overcame the Ottoman siege in 1565, its name was changed to Vittoriosa or 'the victorious city' to commemorate the victory over the Turks.

Hospitaller military operations between the move to Malta and the great siege of 1565 were limited and not entirely successful. Their actions were hampered by France, whose brief alliance with the Ottoman empire not only meant the end of French domination of the Order but sometimes resulted in French brother knights taking part in joint Franco-Ottoman military and naval operations. Wherever possible the Maltese Hospitallers carried on their unrelenting privateering warfare in the Aegean and Mediterranean. In fact the Order still hoped to retake Rhodes, or at least to obtain a better base in Sicily, but Tripoli proved a liability and its loss in 1551 was something of a relief, enabling the Hospitallers to concentrate on strengthening Malta. These improvements in and around Birgu (Vittoriosa) were completed just in time for the great Ottoman assault of 1565. The Englishman Richard Knolles, in his *General Historie of the Turkes...* published several decades later, claimed to quote Sultan Sulayman's justification for attacking Malta. Knolles apparently drew on Ottoman sources via French and other travellers to Istanbul, and the sultan's speech is remarkably similar to Venetian complaints about the Order. Sulayman supposedly described

The Hospitaller fortifications at Bodrum were built to replace Izmir, which fell to Timur-i Lenk in 1402. (Author's photograph)

the brother knights as, 'Crossed pirates which vaunt themselves to be the bulwark of Christendom,' and addressing his followers the sultan continued, 'You yourselves daily hear the pitiful complains of our subjects and merchants, whome these Maltese, I say not soldiers but pirates, if they but look into those seas, spoil and make prizes of, whose injuries to revenge, all laws both of God and men do require.'

The result was an epic siege in which the Ottoman Turks were totally defeated (see Campaign 50, *Malta 1565*). Whether this victory was really a turning point in history is doubtful. It certainly did not destroy or even much damage Ottoman naval or military might. Nor did it change the course of Ottoman expansion. What the great siege of 1565 did do, however, was to revive Hospitaller morale, prestige, recruitment and support within the Catholic Christian world. From that date onwards a new chapter opened in the long history of the Hospitallers.

COLLECTIONS AND MAJOR RELATED SITES

The armour found at Rhodes has been dispersed and some pieces have been lost. Nevertheless the Rhodes armour is particularly important because it is ordinary military kit rather than the splendid examples of the armourer's art that are found in many great museums. It seems to have been the remains of an arsenal largely ignored by the Ottoman Turks because these objects were not the sort of thing used by Ottoman soldiers. The remains included no weapons, however, because these were re-used. The largest number of the pieces of armour were made in northern Italy, while others came from Germany, Flanders, France, England and Iberia. However, identification is largely made on the basis of style, since only a few objects had identifiable armourers' marks. Items from Rhodes are now found in the following museums:

Art Institute (Chicago, USA).
Higgins Armory Museum (Worcester, Mass., USA).
Metropolitan Museum of Art (New York, USA).
Musée d'Armes (Liège, Belgium).
Musée de l'Armée (Paris, France).
Museo Civico (Brescia, Italy).
Museum of Art (Cleveland, USA).
Museum of Art (Philadelphia, USA).
Museum of the Order of St John (London, England).
Royal Armouries (Leeds, England).
Royal Ontario Museum (Toronto, Canada).
Swiss Institute of Arms and Armour (Grandson, Switzerland).

The Museum of the Order of St John in London also has an excellent library which contains the *Rhodes Missal*. The famous Armoury of the Knights in Malta has a superb collection of arms and armour but almost all dates from a later period.

Of all the locations associated with the Order of Hospitallers during the 14th and 15th centuries nothing compares with Rhodes and the neighbouring islands. The following are the most important sites:

Cyprus:
  Kolossi – castle and sugar refinery.
Turkey:
  Bodrum – castle.
  Silifke – castle.
Greece:
  Kálymnos – Pothía, castle; Khorió, castle.
  Kastellórizo – castle.
  Kos – Kos town, castle; Old Pylai, castle; Andimákhia, castle.
  Léros – Plátanos, castle.
  Nísíros – castle.
  Rhodes – fortified city of Rhodes enclosing many other Hospitaller buildings; Lindos, castle; Phileremos, restored Hospitaller church; Arkhangelos, castle; Pharaklos, castle; Alimnia, castle; Kastéllos, castle; Monolithos, castle.
  Simi – Khorió, castle.
  Tílos – Megálo Khorió, castle.

Elsewhere in Europe there are hundreds of sites associated with the Order, ranging from castles to churches, infirmaries, ruined commanderies, ancient barns and other examples of medieval agricultural architecture.

BELOW LEFT **The Master of the Order of the Hospital of St John, L'Isle Adam, with two of his knights serving as guards at the Conclave of Cardinals which elected a former knight of the Order as the new Pope, Clement VII. They appear in a wall painting by Giulio Romano in the Raphael Rooms of the Vatican, painted after 1523. These Hospitallers wear their armour beneath the loose-fitting clothes which were fashionable at that time. (Musei Vaticani Archivio Fotografico, Rome)**

BELOW RIGHT **The master, attended by other members of the Order, directs the activities of local Rhodian Greek craftsmen during the repair of the city's fortifications before the siege of 1480. (*Obsidionis Rhodie Urbis Descriptio*, Bibliothèque Nationale, Ms. Lat. 6067, f.9v, Paris, France)**

FURTHER READING

Acri 1291 – la fine della prezenza degli ordini militari in Terra Santa e i nuovi orientamenti nel XIV secolo, a cura di Francesco Tommasi (*Biblioteca di Militia Sacra 1*), Perugia, 1996

Alliott, E. A., *The Rhodes Missal*, London, 1980

Azzopardi, J. (ed), *The Sovereign Military Order of St. John of Jerusalem, of Rhodes and Malta. The Order's Early Legacy*, Valleta, 1989

Barber, M. C., *The Military Orders; Fighting for the Faith and Caring for the Sick*, Aldershot, 1994

Bradford, E., *The Shield and the Sword; The Knights of St. John, Jerusalem, Rhodes and Malta*, New York, 1972

Coli, E., et al (ed), *Militia Sacra, Gli Ordini militari tra Europe e Terrasanta*, Perugia, 1994

Delaville le Roulx, J. M. A., *Les Hospitaliers à Rhodes (1310–1421)*, Paris, 1913; reprinted London, 1974

Demurger, A., *Les ordres religieux-militaires de la première croisade a Lepante*, Paris, 1999

Forey, A. J., *The Military Orders from the Twelfth to the Early Fourteenth Centuries*, London, 1991

Forey, A. J., *Military Orders and Crusaders*, London, 1994

Hunyadi, Z., 'The Hungarian nobility and the Knights of St. John', in N. Tonnerre (ed), *La noblesse dans les territoires angevin a la fin du Moyen Age*, Ecole Française de Rome, Rome, 2000

Josserand, M. P., 'La figure du commandeur dans les prieures castillans et leonais du Temple et de l'Hopital: une approche prosopographique (fin XII-milieu XIVs)', in *Ordens Militares, Guerra, Religiao Poder e Cultura – Actas do III Encontro sobre Ordens Militares*, Vol I, Lisbon 1999

Karcheski, W. J. and T. Richardson, *The Medieval Armour from Rhodes*, Leeds & Worcester Mass., 2000

The Hospitaller castle on Lango (now called Kos) largely dates from the 14th century, though the 15th-century additions are visible on the left. (Photograph National Library of Malta)

Kedar, B. Z., *The Franks in the Levant, 11th to 14th centuries*, reprints London, 1993

Laking, G. F., *A Catalogue of the Armour and Arms in the Armoury of the Knights of St. John of Jerusalem Now in the Palace, Valetta, Malta*, London, n.d.

Les Ordres Militaires, la vie rurales et le peuplement en Europe occidentale (XII-XVIIIe siecle) (Sixieme Journees internationales d'histoire 21–23 septembre 1984), Flaran VI 1984), Auch, 1986

Luttrell, A., (ed), *Medieval Malta: Studies in Malta before the Knights*, London, 1975

    The Hospitallers in Cyprus, Rhodes, Greece and the West (1291–1440), London, 1978

    Latin Greece, the Hospitallers and the Crusades 1291–1440, Aldershot, 1982

    The Hospitallers of Rhodes and their Mediterranean World, Aldershot, 1992

    The Hospitaller State on Rhodes and its Western Provinces, Aldershot, 1999

Mallia-Milanes, V. (ed), *Hospitaller Malta 1530–1798*, Malta, 1993

Nicholson, H. J. (ed), *The Military Orders, Volume 2. Welfare and Warfare*, Cardiff, 1998

Riley-Smith, J., *Hospitallers: The History of the Order of St. John*, London, 1999

    The Knights of St. John in Jerusalem and Cyprus 1050–1310, London, 1967

Selwood, D., *Knights of the Cloister, Templars and Hospitallers in central-southern Occitania 1100–1300*, Woodbridge, 1999

Sire, H. J. A., *The Knights of Malta*, New Haven, 1994

Topping, P., *Studies in Latin Greece AD 1205–1715*, London, 1977

An early 19th-century engraving of the Palace of the Masters of the Order of Hospitallers in Rhodes, as it appeared before 1856.

GLOSSARY

(Also see Glossary in Warrior 33, *Knight Hospitaller (1) 1100–1306*)

Admiral Senior naval officer in the Order.
Aketon Quilted garment worn beneath armour.
Almain collar Style of plated gorget.
Armet Form of helmet consisting of several hinged pieces.
Arming cap Padded cap worn beneath a helmet.
Arming doublet or **arming jacket** Garment worn beneath armour, often with elements of mail attached.
Arming points Laces on inner layer of armour or clothing to which plate armour is tied.
Armourer's mark Stamp on a piece of armour indicating the manufacturer.
Aspirant Novice wishing to become a full brother of the Order.
Auberge Dormitory or barracks.
Aventail Mail attached to a helmet to protect neck and shoulders.
Bascinet Close-fitting helmet.
Basilard Form of large dagger.
Beylik Small, independent Turkish Islamic state.
Bevor Piece of armour attached to front of helmet to protect throat (*see also* wrapper).
Bill Form of long-hafted infantry weapon.
Breviary Book containing the religious services for each day.

Brigandine Form of scale-lined body armour.
Buckler Small hand-held shield.
Buonavoglia Volunteer galley oarsman.
Calcar Raised extension or beak on the prow of a galley.
Carovane Military service or expedition, including naval service.
Castellan Officer in command of an important castle.
Chancellor Senior legal official.
Chantry priest Priest reciting Mass for the dead.
Chapel-de-fer Brimmed helmet.
Chapter Meeting of a convent or of executive members of the Order.
Chapter General Meeting of senior officials of the Order.
Chausse Mail leg protection.
Cinquedea Very broad short sword.
Close helmet Style of helmet with pivoted front part and pivoted visor.
Coat-of-plates Early form of laminated or scale-lined body armour.
Coif Head covering, of cloth or mail.
Collachio Inner part of the city of Rhodes reserved for the Order.
Collière Neck and shoulder protection, usually of mail.
Commander Officer in charge of a Hospitaller commandery.
Commander of knights Officer who led the knights if the marshal or his lieutenant were not available.
Commandery Smallest territorial division of the Order (*see also* Preceptory).

The Hospitaller brethren who defended the Order's new base on Malta against the Ottomans in 1565 were equipped with largely Italian arms and armour. These are fine examples of the Italian fashion. (Museo Stibbert, Florence, Italy)

Convent Grouping of Hospitaller brethren, usually referring to the central convent or headquarters.

Conventual prior The Order's most senior religious official.

Couter Elbow protection.

Cuisse Protection for the thigh, usually quilted.

Domus Individual house within the Order.

Donat Noblemen waiting to join the Hospitallers as a full brother.

Drapier Official in charge of clothing.

Falchion Broad single-edged sword.

Fauld Lower part of a plated cuirass covering abdomen and hips.

Fausse-braie Low defensive wall ahead of the main fortification.

Galiote Small galley.

Gorget Plated protection for the throat.

Grand commander Master's administrative second in command.

Grand preceptor Senior official in charge of priories in Germany, central Europe and sometimes Scandinavia.

Great carrack Large sailing ship.

Greave Armour for the lower leg.

Guisarme Infantry staff weapon with a long blade.

Hand-and-a-half sword Large sword that can be wielded with two hands.

Haubergeon Small mail hauberk.

Hauberk Mail armour for the body and usually the arms.

Helm Large helmet usually enclosing the entire head.

Hospice Hostel, often for pilgrims.

Hospitaller Official responsible for the sick.

Infirmarian Official in charge of the infirmary.

Infirmary Hospital in the modern sense.

Jupon Tight-fitting quilted garment, originally worn beneath armour.

Langue Basic linguistic division of the Order.

Latten Metal alloy similar to brass.

Magistri muratores Senior builders, usually Greek in Rhodes.

Maisons-Dieu Hospitals run by city authorities.

Marshal The most senior military official in the Order.

Missal Book of the Mass.

Mitten Protection for the hand without individual fingers.

Mitten gauntlet Plated protection for the hand without separate fingers.

Nauclerius Sailing master aboard a ship, but not its captain.

Novitiate System of training youngsters for entry into a religious order.

Pauldron Plated armour for shoulder.

Pilier Senior figure in a langue or linguistic division of the Order.

Plackart Plate armour for the abdomen, usually worn in addition to a cuirass.

Pole-arm Infantry weapon with a long staff.

Poleyn Protection for the knee.

Preceptor Official in command of a preceptory.

Preceptory Smallest territorial and administrative unit in the Order (see also Commandery).

Priory Administrative province of the Hospitaller Order.

Privy Lavatory.

Proctor Legal and disciplinary official.

Proctor general Senior proctor in the Order.

Procurator Senior legal and financial official.

Psalter Book of Psalms.

Refectory Dining hall.

Rerebrace Armour for the upper arm.

Rondel dagger Dagger in which the guard and pommel are in the form of discs.

Sabaton Armour for the foot.

Salet Open-faced helmet also covering the rear of the head.

Servitudo marina Obligation to serve in the Order's galleys.

Stabilimenta Legislation within the Order.

Statute A law of the Order.

Studium College or place of study.

Surcoat Large garment worn over armour, usually heraldic.

Tabard Small garment worn over armour, usually heraldic.

Tersenal Naval arsenal of the Order at Rhodes.

Tippet Large piece of mail armour protecting throat, shoulders and upper part of the chest.

Turcopole Locally recruited light cavalry soldier of Near Eastern origin; earlier of Middle Eastern origin.

Turcopolier Senior officer in command of the Order's turcopoles.

Vambrace Armour for the lower arm.

Vervelles Pierced studs through which an aventail is laced to a helmet.

Wrapper Piece of armour attached to front of helmet to protect throat (see also bevor).

Some Renaissance portraits of young men wearing the Hospitaller cross give a more romantic than religious impression. This painting is by Giorgione and probably dates from the end of the 15th century. (Uffizi Gallery, Florence, Italy)

THE COLOUR PLATES

A: WAR AT SEA, MID-14TH CENTURY

Two Hospitaller galleys have captured a Turkish ship. One Hospitaller brother knight is holding on to a captured Turkish boy, unsure whether he is old enough to be killed. There was no Hospitaller uniform as such during the 14th or even 15th centuries, though a scarlet surcoat with its eight-pointed cross served this purpose. Written sources, supported by the relatively small amount of pictorial material relating directly to the Hospitallers, indicates that brethren-in-arms used a great variety of military equipment, mostly manufactured in Italy. An increasing amount of individual decoration also seems to have been permitted. The brother knight shown here has a deep form of iron bascinet with tiny rivets to hold the internal lining. His mail hauberk has a stiffened collar, and over this he wears a fabric-covered coat-of-plates which is probably lined with hardened leather scales. The similarly fabric-covered rerebraces on his arms would have had iron splints inside. The padded mail gauntlets seem to enclose a draw-string, perhaps to tighten them around his wrists. The leg protection consists of linen-covered cuisses with brass rivets securing internal scales or splints, massive iron poleyns over his knees, iron greaves that only cover the front part of his legs, with mail chausses beneath these. The brother knight is armed with a basilard form of dagger and a sword.

A second Hospitaller brother sergeant to his right wears a mail tippet over his neck and shoulders and a coat-of-plates secured by a bolt and loops on the right shoulder only. The fabric of the coat-of-plates would originally have been red but has here faded almost to brown. Hardened leather rerebraces protect his upper arms, while splinted iron vambraces protect his lower arms, in addition to which he has a mid-sleeved mail hauberk. The only protection on his legs are quilted cuisses. He is armed with a large, grooved falchion. In addition, he wears an iron chapel-de-fer with a very deep brim.

A sailor with a large staff weapon is dividing the captives (among them a Greek marine to his right, a Turk to his left, and a Turkish woman) into two groups, Orthodox and Muslim Turks: the former will be enslaved, the latter killed and thrown overboard.

B: BROTHER KNIGHT-IN-ARMS C.1330

1 Brother knight with Anglo-French-style arms and armour.
2 Middle layer of armour consisting of a mail collière partly covered in latten scales (2a), a cloth-covered coat-of-plates (2b), linen-covered quilted cuisses (2c) and hardened leather greaves on the front of the legs with integral sabatons (2d).
3 Inner layer of protection showing the bottom of the linen-covered quilted aketon and one of the greaves.
4 Detail of the visored helm showing section and interior with the separated visor seen from the front.
5 Detail of the mail coif showing the padded lining of the skull secured by a decorated leather brow-band, plus a rear view showing the laced slit to secure this coif close to head and neck.
6 Detail of the guisarme (also shown disassembled).
7 Detail of disassembled dagger.

Firearms became a vital aspect of warfare during the early 16th century and the Hospitallers adopted them with enthusiasm. (*In situ*, Maison d'Adam et Eve, Beaulieu sur Dordogne, France; author's photograph)

8 Detail of sheath for the dagger, also shown from the rear.
9 The gauntlet showing the stiff leather or rawhide wrist and soft-leather basic glove.
10 Front, rear and cross section (10a) of a buckler or small shield showing the large iron boss, a layer of leather across the front, two layers of wood with crossing grain, and large wooden grip.
11 Detail of sword, also shown disassembled.
12 Detail of scabbard lacing showing the two upper thongs of the front part of the sword-belt around the scabbard and tied to themselves.
13 Detail of belt decoration and strap-end.
14 Detail of poleyns showing the iron frame riveted to the hardened leather knee-cop with a soft leather lining.
15 Detail of coat-of-plates with the right shoulder unlaced and part of the brown cloth covering torn back to show metal scales. 15a shows the exterior of the shoulder lacing, and 15b shows the interior.
16 Detail of one of the greaves showing two layers of hardened leather over the shins and hardened leather lames of the integral sabatons.
17 Gilded bronze rower spurs with leather straps, gilded buckle and strap end.
18 Interior of shield, entirely covered in leather. A cross section showing the curvature is detailed above this.

C: A PRECEPTOR TOURING HIS ESTATE, C.1375

The brother preceptor is on horseback and is talking to some peasants on his estate in Provence. The large black felt beret remained a basic element of a Hospitaller's attire when not in armour. Otherwise clothes were of a sombre colour beneath the traditional black woollen cape, here lacking a hood, with a white Hospitaller cross on its left shoulder. Some pictorial sources also show metallic crosses at the ends of the cords that would close the neck of the cloak. Some element of decoration in horse harnesses was also now acceptable.

To his left is a brother sergeant-at-arms. Only the man's tight-fitting surcoat identifies him as a Hospitaller. Otherwise his southern French or northern-Italian style armour consists of an iron bascinet, a mail collière that extends quite far down his shoulders, a long-sleeved mail hauberk without mittens, iron couters on his elbows, linen-covered cuisses over his thighs, and iron poleyns and greaves without sabatons. He is armed with a large basilard dagger and a short infantry sword.

D: BROTHER KNIGHT, C.1430

1   Brother knight in Milanese armour. This was the latest, most fashionable and probably the most expensive form of protection during the period. Perhaps only senior men of the Order could have afforded it. His helmet is of the close-fitting armet form and is worn above a mail collière. The basic cuirass is largely covered with a tabard bearing the insignia of the Order. The pauldrons over his shoulders are different for the right and left sides, while his arms are almost entirely enclosed in riveted, hinged and buckled plates. His legs are similarly enclosed except that his feet are only protected by a flap of mail that does not seem to cover his toes.

2   Armet-type helmet shown with its visor raised, with a throat-covering bevor attached, and from the rear with one of the hinged side-pieces raised.

3   Detail of the vervelles on an armet showing a cord threaded though the vervelles and a strip of pierced leather over them.

4   Detail of the sword, and richly decorated gilded bronze hilt.

5   Front and side views of the rondel-style dagger with front and rear views of the sheath, and details of attachment to the belt (5a).

6   Oval shield with four rivets to secure holding straps, perhaps for combat on foot. Cross sections from the top and side are also shown.

7   Pole-arm with thrusting spike, hooked spike, and four toothed pick. A top view of the head of the pole-arm is also shown (7a).

8   Side profile of iron leg armour.

Two portraits of anonymous men wearing two different styles of protection over which they would place their plate armour, by Moroni, Italian mid-16th century. The figure on the left wears an arming doublet, while the man of the right seems to have a long-sleeved mail haubergeon beneath his doublet. (National Gallery, London, England)

Although the 15th century has been described as the high-point in western European plate armour, other forms of protection were still worn beneath such 'white harness'. These could include a quilted jupon or arming jacket (9), here shown with pairs of leather laces or arming points that would be trimmed short once tied to various items of armour, plus a short-sleeved mail haubergeon (10), and a mail collière with an apparently stiffened neck (11). Leg armour was put on before the hauberk and cuirass. The plate cuirass itself (12) consisted of a breastplate, backplate and the upwards overlapping lames or hoops of the fauld that protected his abdomen. An additional strip of mail, sometimes with a decorative edge, could be added to the lowest lame. These items combined to create a formidable inner layer of protection (13).

E: THE HOSPITALLERS DEFEND RHODES FROM THE MAMLUK FLEET, 1444

Artillery was now playing an increasingly important role in siege warfare, and the Hospitallers clearly took a great interest in the latest technological advances. Here the master of the Order, Fr Jean Bonpar de Lastic (second from left), is inspecting a battery of four cannon which are on a raised mound of earth, supported by timber planking. This enabled the cannons to fire over the defensive wall. The master is accompanied by a brother sergeant (who carries the long, large-bladed guisarme) and a turcopole of the Order (far left), while the gunnery team includes local resident militiamen and a master gunner, who directs proceedings from behind the battery.

F: ARMING A BROTHER KNIGHT, C.1500

Several manuscript illustrations and other pictorial sources show the process of arming a knight or man-at-arms in the later medieval period. These are supported by a smaller number of detailed descriptions. Apart from the sword, the pieces of armour shown around the brother knight and his squire were all found in Rhodes where they once formed part of the Order's armoury.

The brother knight being armed is based on a southern German carving that illustrates an unusual form of mail garment incorporating a close breech or breeches of mail. These would have been used when fighting on foot, and included a laced mail flap that permitted the wearer to relieve himself. He also wears what appears to be a form of padded arming cap, while his young squire ties the arming points that secure his left leg harness. Other such pairs of laces secured other items of armour.

Inset around the two figures are the following items:
1. An armet helmet, perhaps Italian, c.1500–1515, considerably restored (private collection).
2. A visor for an armet helmet, probably Milanese, c.1500–1510, all-iron (Royal Armouries, inv. IV.437, Leeds).
3. Bevor or wrapper for an armet helmet, probably Italian, c.1500–1510 (Royal Armouries, inv. III.1147, Leeds).
4. Salet helmet, Milanese, c.1490–1500 (Royal Armouries, inv. IV.24, Leeds).
5. Backplate, Milanese, with a stamped armourer's mark (below), attributed to Giovanni Antonio delle Fibbie (Royal Armouries, inv. III.1093, Leeds).

The main gate of what was originally the Hospitaller Priory of Clerkenwell in London was rebuilt in 1504, less than 40 years before the dissolution of the monasteries ended the Hospitallers' presence in England. The Order was subsequently revived in an Anglican form and St John's Gate now forms part of the headquarters of this Order. (Photograph Museum of the Order of St John)

6. Plackart, Italian, c.1475–1500, partially restored with a later tongued buckle on the right side (Higgins Armory Museum, inv. 3127.9, Worcester, Mass.).
7. Breastplate, Italian, c.1490–1500, partially restored (Royal Armouries, inv. III.1083, Leeds).
8. Vambrace, probably Italian, c.1500 (Royal Armouries, inv. III.1111–1112, Leeds).
9. Rear of pauldron for right shoulder, Milanese, c.1490–1500, with an armourer's mark shown below (Royal Armouries, inv. III.1121, Leeds).
10. Mitten gauntlet for left hand, probably Italian c.1500, the articulating rivets on the sides of the knuckles originally had brass caps (Royal Armouries, inv. III.1108, Leeds).
11. Cuisse, poleyn and greave for left leg, northern Italian c.1500–1510, restored: several rivets and all leather straps and buckles are modern replacements (Royal Armouries, inv. III.1126–1127, Leeds).
12. Hand-and-a-half sword from Slebech Abbey, early 15th century (Order of St John, Priory for Wales, on loan to National Museum of Wales, inv. 33.106, Cardiff).

G: HERALDRY OF THE MASTERS 1306–1565, AND A BROTHER KNIGHT IN FULL CEREMONIAL DRESS C.1525

The Hospitaller brother knight is dressed as a guard in Rome. The very bulky appearance of this figure is a result of the full armour beneath his fashionably 'puffed' loose-fitting clothing. The full plate armour includes the same basic elements as seen earlier, though lacking gauntlets. A mail collière has, however, been replaced by a fluted and laminated plate gorget to protect his throat. He also wears a thickly quilted and decorated arming cap beneath his hat. His dagger is of the eared form which originated in Islamic Granada, while the complex hilt of his sword incorporates a horizontal ring to protect his forefinger. The helmet beneath his arm is a visored salet.

Also shown are coats-of-arms of the masters of the Order in Rhodes, Viterbo and Malta to 1568:

1   Foulques de Villaret (1305–1317).
(Two year gap under a temporary lieutenant, Gerard de Pins)
2   Hélion de Villeneuve (1319–1346).
3   Dieudonné de Gozon (1346–1353).
4   Pierre de Corneillan (1353–1355).
5   Roger de Pins (1355–1365).
6a and 6b Raimond Bèrenger (1365–1374); several arms are attributed to him, these being the most common.
7   Robert de Juilly (1374–1377).
8   Juan Fernandez de Heredia (1377–1396).

9   Philibert de Naillac (1396–1421).
10 Antonio de Fluvia (1421–1437).
11 Jean de Lastic (1437–1454).
12 Jacques de Milly (1454–1461).
13 Raimundo Zacosta (1461–1467).
14 Giovan Battista Orsini (1467–1476).
15 Pierre d'Aubusson (1476–1503); from now on the master's arms were quartered with the red and white cross of the Order.
16 Emery d'Amboise, called Chaumont (1503–1512).
17 Guy de Blanchefort (1512–1513).
18 Fabrizio del Carretto (1513–1521).
19 Philippe Villiers de l'Isle Adam (1521–1534).
20 Pietrino del Ponte (1534–1535).
21 Didier de Tholon Sainte-Jalle (1535–1536).
22 Juan de Homedes y Coscon (1536–1553).
23 Claude de la Sengle (1553–1557).
24 Jean Parisot de la Valette (1557–1568).

H: INVESTITURE OF TWO NOVITIATES AS FULL BRETHREN OF THE ORDER, MID-16TH CENTURY

The continuity of Hospitaller traditions and religious ceremonial is clearly shown in their investiture ceremony. A detailed written description from the early 14th century, for example, is identical to a ceremony illustrated in a late 16th-century engraving. Here two other brother knights watch the ceremony. One is wearing a buff leather arming doublet. Relatively small pieces of mail are laced to this doublet to protect his otherwise vulnerable armpits when wearing full armour. The other brother knight is wearing a long-sleeved mail haubergeon beneath his jacket, plus a plated gorget of a type known as an almain collar. He carries a typical mid-16th century close helmet.

The defeat of the Ottoman Sultan Sulayman's attempt to conquer the new Hospitaller base on Malta in 1565 revived the Order's morale and prestige. This is one of Matteo Perez d'Aleccio's preliminary modellos for his famous wall paintings in the Grand Master's Palace in Valetta. (National Maritime Museum, London, England)

INDEX

Figures in **bold** refer to illustrations

Alexandria, Hospitaller conquest of (1365) 6
Aringhierre, Alberto **21**
armour and clothing 10, **19**, 22-5, **24**, **27**, 28, **29**, 45, **51**, 58, 60, 61-2, **61**, 62, **B**, **D**, **F**
Arnau de Soler, Fr 11

Bandini, Fr Melchiore 47
bascinets **10**
Bela IV (king of Hungary) 14
Birgu 53
Bodrum, castle and fortifications 17, 50, **53**
Bosredon, Pierre de **17**

cannons 23
Caoursin, Guillaume 31, 47
carovane (naval service) 31
Carretto, Fabrizio del 50
Castellorizzo 50
Cervellon, Ugo de **8**
Charles V (king of Spain) 52
Clement VI (Pope) 19
Clement VII (Pope) 50-1
Clerkenwell Priory 62

d'Aubusson, Pierre **14**
de Gagnac, Fr Bertrin 21
de Geoffroi, Fr Antoine 47
Destan of Umur Pasha 29, 32
Dieudonné de Gozon 19, 49
donats 11

Edward III (king of England) 18

fencing 28
Fiore dei Liberi 28
firearms **60**
fortifications 17, 49-50, **50**, **55**
Foulques de Villaret 4
Fransières, Fr Jean de 47

galleys **28**, 30-1, 32, **32**
Gulf of Iskenderun, defeat of Mamluk fleet in (1510) 27

Helion de Villeneuve 5
Henry IV (king of England) 11
Henry VIII (king of England) 23
Heredia, Juan Fernandez de **15**, **18**, 46
Hill, Johan 25
Hospitallers
    brother knights **9**, 11, **21**, 60, 61-2, **B**, **D**, **F**
    brother sergeants 11-13

carvings **12**
castles 55
commanderies 43
crosses 59
effigies 6, **8**, **12**, **45**
fighting methods 28, 29
finances 17-18
heraldry 63, **G**
infirmaries 44-6
langues (tongues) 10, 13
lawyers 42
Malta, move to 50-4
naval warfare 26-8, 31-2
novitiates 11, 63, **H**
possessions 14-15, 16, **28**
preceptors 15, 16, 61, **C**
priories **7**, 13, **62**
prisoners of 19-20, 44
recruitment 9-13
religious relics 19
Rhodes, conquest of (1306-9) 4-6
Rhodes, defence of (1444) 62, **E**
robes 18, 22
scholarly activities 46-7
seals 11
strategy 26
support services 41-2
Huss, Ulrich de **45**

Izmir see Smyrna

Jaime (king of Aragon's son), initiation into the Order 11

Knolles, Richard 53
Kolossi castle **41**
Kos castle **56**

Lily, William 46
L'Isle Adam 55
Louis (king of France), landing at Damietta **22**

magistri muratores 50
Malta
    Hospitaller move to 50-4
    infirmary 46
    Ottoman siege of (1565) 53-4, **63**
Mamluks 4, 6, 26, 27, 29, 43
manuscripts **44**
Margrave of Brandenburg 51
Mertola castle **8**
Mézières, Philip de 20
Mont Joye (ship) 41
Morelli, Jean 50

naval warfare 26-8, **28**, 31-2, **32**, 60, **A**
physicians 45, **46**
Pigafetta, Fr Antonio 47
Pigot, John 17
piliers 13, 44
probi homines 45
Puenta de la Reinha **16**

Quiton, Fr Jean 47

Renart the Fox **4**
Rhodes
    the collachio 43
    conquest by Hospitallers (1306-9) 4-6
    earthquake (1481) **20**
    fortifications 17, 49-50, **50**, **55**
    Hospitallers' defence of (1444) 62, **E**
    infirmary 44-6, **48**
    Palace of the Masters **57**
    siege of (1444) 29
    siege of (1480) **14**, **31**, **52**
    Street of the Knights **17**
    Tower of Master de Naillac 49-50
Rhodes Missal 17, 54
Roger de Pins 10, 44

Sabba da Castiglione, Fr 47
St Peter, castle of **30**
St William, martyrdom of **26**
saddlery 42
Santa Anna (carrack) 32
Sanudo, Marino 20
servitudo marina 6, 19
Silifke castle **5**
Smyrna (Izmir), seizure of (1344) 5-6
stabilimenta 16
Sulayman, Sultan 53-4
swords 28, **49**

Templars, disbandment 5, 9, 13
Teutonic Knights 4, 10, 20
Tirant lo Blanc 29, 32
turcopoles 13

Valette, Jean Parisot de la 22, 53
Villegaignon, Fr Nicholas Durand de 47
Vimercate, Gaspare da **52**

Ward, Stephen 13
warrior saints **9**, **12**, 14

Zacchia, Fr Laudivio 47

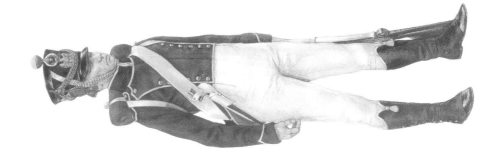

FIND OUT MORE ABOUT OSPREY

❏ Please send me the latest listing of Osprey's publications

❏ I would like to subscribe to Osprey's e-mail newsletter

Title / rank

Name

Address

City / county

Postcode / zip   state / country

e-mail

WAR

I am interested in:

❏ Ancient world
❏ Medieval world
❏ 16th century
❏ 17th century
❏ 18th century
❏ Napoleonic
❏ 19th century

❏ American Civil War
❏ World War 1
❏ World War 2
❏ Modern warfare
❏ Military aviation
❏ Naval warfare

Please send to:

North America:
Osprey Direct, c/o Random House Distribution Center,
400 Hahn Road, Westminster, MD 21157, USA

UK, Europe and rest of world:
Osprey Direct UK, P.O. Box 140, Wellingborough,
Northants, NN8 2FA, United Kingdom

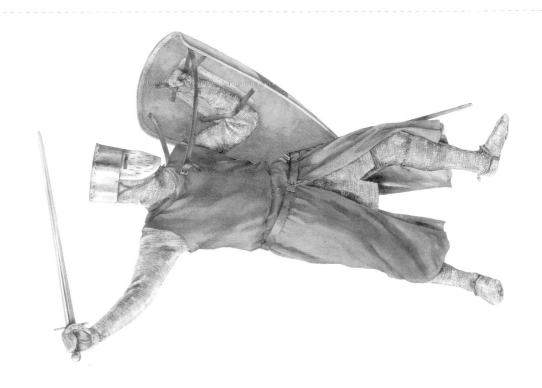

OSPREY
PUBLISHING

Young Guardsman
Figure taken from Warrior 22:
Imperial Guardsman 1799–1815
Published by Osprey
Illustrated by Richard Hook

www.ospreypublishing.com

Knight, c.1190
Figure taken from Warrior 1: *Norman Knight 950 – 1204 AD*
Published by Osprey
Illustrated by Christa Hook

POSTCARD